Cyprus

D0487165

Berlitz Publishing Company, Inc.

Princeton   Mexico City   London   Eschborn   Singapore

Text:	Revised and updated by Paul Murphy
Editor:	Erica Spaberg Keirstead
Photography:	Paul Murphy, pages 3, 4, 6, 8, 11, 12, 14, 17, 18, 28, 32, 38, 41, 42, 45, 48, 52, 65, 66, 68, 71, 72, 75, 76, 79, 81, 83, 85, 86, 88, 90, 100; Jon Davison, pages 20, 24, 26, 31, 35, 51, 55, 58, 62, 92
Cover Photo:	Paul Murphy
Photo Editor:	Naomi Zinn
Layout:	Media Content Marketing, Inc.
Cartography:	Raffaele Degennaro

The author would like to thank Sonja Firth (CIB) and the Cyprus Tourism Organization; Le Meridien Hotel, Limassol; George Gregoriou, Kiniras Hotel, Paphos; and Exalt Travel.

Although the publisher tries to insure the accuracy of all the information in this book, changes are inevitable and errors may result. The publisher cannot be responsible for any resulting loss, inconvenience, or injury. If you find an error in this guide, please let the editors know by writing to Berlitz Publishing Company, 400 Alexander Park, Princeton, NJ 08540-6306.

A word about place names: In 1994, Cypriot authorities introduced a new system of place names. In keeping with the policy of most tour operators, publishers, and other bodies throughout the world who are connected with tourism on Cyprus, this guide continues to use the familiar pre-1994 place names.

ISBN 2-8315-7167-7

Revised 1999

Printed in Italy
040/104 RP

CONTENTS

• A ☛ in the text denotes a highly recommended sight

Cyprus

CYPRUS AND THE CYPRIOTS

Cyprus made its ancient fortune from copper, a chunk of history that's echoed today in the colors that make up the Republic's national flag. In modern times, Cyprus's greatest natural resource is sunshine, around 340 days every year, which has encouraged its development into one of Europe's holiday hotspots. Cyprus is particularly popular with the British, who contribute roughly half of all its visitors. Yet despite its label as "Aphrodite's island," most of those who flock to this sun-soaked Mediterranean outpost are unlikely to find love at first sight. No one can pretend that Cyprus has the obvious appeal (or architecture) of an intimate, whitewashed Greek island, nor the immediate stunning natural scenery of Corfu. And most of its resorts, it has to be said, are large and busy, over-commercialized, and with little obvious historical or cultural character. But you don't have to delve too far to start to appreciate this island. In fact, its charms will probably come to you, most obviously in the shape of its remarkable people.

Considering their turbulent and traumatic recent history, you have to marvel at the Cypriots' quiet, easygoing nature. This is, after all, an island that was invaded by Turkey and split in two in 1974. At a stroke, some 170,000 Greek Cypriots became refugees in their own country, and were forced to flee to the south of the island. At the same time, around 30,000 Turkish Cypriots moved in the opposite direction. The island is still divided today, and policed by the UN, a political solution that's just as difficult as in any of the world's most contested territories.

Although it's possible to visit the north (an area that only Turkey recognizes as a separate republic), most travelers

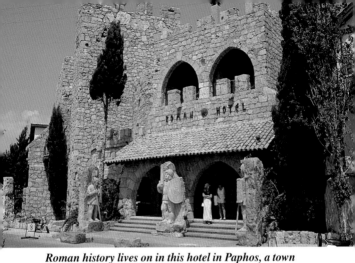

Roman history lives on in this hotel in Paphos, a town rejuvenated since the tourist boom of the 1970s.

choose the Greek-influenced south. But for the intrepid who do venture across the line that separates the two regions of the island, the Turkish north offers up a much less commercialized landscape, including some pristine beaches and many more varieties of flora and fauna.

Yet through it all, the Greek Cypriots have managed to retain the sunny disposition you may expect (though don't always find) in the Mediterranean. As many travelers know, the Greeks are by nature a friendly, easy-going, hospitable people. Yet the Cypriots seem to take this a stage further. Ask a couple harvesting grapes if you can take their photograph, and they will not only strike a happy pose, but also gather a large bag of grapes especially for you to take home. Compliment a young chef on the quality of his *sheftalia* at a *taverna* and chat to him about modern village life, and he will insist that lunch is on the house. Chat happily to an old man about Makarios and EOKA days, only to notice some 15 minutes later that he has left his family waiting in the car (engine still running!) in order to talk to a complete stranger. Of course,

The Lay of the Land

Tucked into the far northeast corner of the Mediterranean between Turkish Anatolia and Syria, Cyprus is the Mediterranean's third largest island, after Sicily and Sardinia. (To put its size into perspective, Cyprus is roughly half the size of Wales.)

Its land surface of 9,251 km2 (3,572 sq. miles) sandwiches the broad Mesaoria Plain between two chains of mountains — the Kyrenia (or Pentadaktylos "Five Fingers") range in the northeast and the Troodos range in the southwest. Three major rivers — running dry in summer — originate in the Troodos mountains: the Pedieos flowing east to Famagusta Bay, the Karyoti west to Morphou Bay, and the Kouris south to Episkopi. The highest peak is Mount Olympus in the Troodos range, at 1,951 m (6,401 ft).

Population
741,000 in the south; 171,000 in the Turkish-occupied north, including 80,000 post-1974 settlers from Anatolia and 35,000 Turkish soldiers.

Capital
Nicosia: 193,000 in the Greek-Cypriot city; 41,000 in the Turkish-Cypriot sector (northern Nicosia).

Major Cities
South: Limassol (151,200), Larnaca (67,300), Paphos (37,300), North: Famagusta (21,330), Morphou (11,180), Kyrenia (7,580).

you will have your own experiences, but it is rare that a visitor leaves Cyprus without some tale of the people's generosity.

It is not a mere marketing gimmick that at the end of many a meal, coffee and a liqueur (even if it is the throat-charring *sivania*) is provided "on the house." As you will probably hear said more than once, "it is our custom." You don't have to go to the most remote mountain village for such hospitality, but it is also a truism that you are much less likely to find such warmth in the more obvious tourist-oriented watering holes.

This widespread cheerfulness is coupled with a dignity that shuns expansive Latin gestures. The British like to think that their presence on the island over the past century has been at least partly responsible, and as far as the politeness of the police and the sober honesty of public officials are concerned, they may be right. But the courtesy of the Cypriots in general seems to be a more deeply ingrained quality.

A more somber note is struck when the question of the divided island is raised. Greek Cypriot refugees from the north react with more melancholy than anger. Nostalgically, restaurants and shops in Larnaca or Limassol may bear the names of their lost homes in Famagusta, Kyrenia, or Bellapais.

Sadly, because of its geographical position, Cyprus has always been in a sea of troubles, continually beset by unwelcome visitors. The ancient myth is that Aphrodite, goddess of love, was born here, and ever since, it seems, everyone has wanted a piece of her island. Apart from attracting Phoenician and Assyrian pirates, conquerors from Egypt and Persia, aggressive Greeks and Turks, Cyprus has been the easy prey of French crusaders and Venetian and Genoese merchants. It was even a pawn in the last days of the British Empire. In his book *Bitter Lemons*, the novelist Lawrence Durrell, who spent time in Cyprus as a teacher and colonial official, revealed just how paternalistic even the best-intentioned British observer could be in the fateful 1950s.

But for today's visitors, who are welcomed with open arms, the traces of the past are one of the most compelling reasons for coming. There are the ancient Greek temples of Kourion and Salamis, the splendid Roman mosaics at Paphos, the crusader castles of Kolossi and the Kyrenia Mountains, the Gothic churches and walled city of Famagusta, the Venetian bastions of Nicosia, and the Byzantine monasteries and churches of the Troodos Mountains.

Although in some ways Cyprus may appear quite British, in others, it can also be a very foreign, exotic place. Perhaps nothing illustrates the contrasts better than the juxtaposition of Turkish mosques (which appear in all the big towns north and south) with the most recent and coziest of historical relics, the humble British pillar box (repainted yellow).

The Troodos Mountains offer a landscape as rich as an ancient treasure chest.

Cyprus is also a country of largely unsung natural beauty. While the resort beaches cater to vacationers who are happy to lie baking in serried ranks, the coastline, particularly of the Akamas Peninsula, has enough rugged cliffs and surf-beaten coves to appeal to the romantic individualist or rugged off-road biker. The Troodos Mountains are a wild and spectacularly verdant adventure of hairpin curves and dense green forest as far as the eye can see.

A Cypriot couple takes a break from harvesting grapes to indulge a photographer.

Sprinkled like forgotten gems among the virgin landscape are tiny Byzantine churches, secrets known only to their immediate parishioners for centuries. Today, nine of these are on the UNESCO protected list, representatives of a pinnacle of artistic achievement. Certainly no visit to Cyprus is complete without making the pilgrimage to at least one of them.

Meanwhile, in the plains of the interior, villages untouched by tourism nestle among olive groves and citrus orchards, and goats and sheep scamper among forgotten ancient ruins. Vineyards climb the sunny hillsides, cypress trees frame a somnolent abbey or the skeleton of an abandoned fortress, and rural Cypriot life continues at a snail's pace.

A BRIEF HISTORY

The first records of human presence in Cyprus seem to be those of a group who were visitors rather than permanent residents. Tools and butchered animal bones found in a cave on the south coast are dated at about 8500 B.C.; the bones are thought to be the remains of pygmy hippopotamus killed and barbecued on the beach by a group of seafarers who landed briefly on the island.

The earliest traces of permanent settlers are sturdy stone bee-hive-shaped dwellings at the northern tip of the Karpas peninsula and at the inland site of Khirokitia in the south, which date back to at least 7000 B.C.

Copper and the First Greeks

By 3500 B.C., copper was being mined in the Troodos foothills and gave the island its first wealth. Cyprus began to prosper as a trading center, with goods coming in from Asia, Egypt, Crete, the Peloponnese, and the Aegean Islands in exchange for Cypriot pottery, copperware, and opium.

After 1600 B.C., large numbers of fortresses were built around the island, which suggests a period of conflict. Copper was sent to mighty Egypt as protection money and, in exchange, the Pharaoh called the king of Cyprus "brother."

Upheaval in the Peloponnese, caused variously by natural calamities and invasions from the north, drove Mycenaean Greeks east across the Mediterranean, and some settled in Cyprus. From 1200 B.C., they established city-kingdoms at Enkomi, replaced later by Salamis (near modern Famagusta), Kition (now Larnaca), Kourion and Paphos in the south, and Soloi and Lapithos in the north. The island acquired the predominantly Greek identity it was never to relinquish. Temples were erected near smelting workshops, presided over by Aphrodite, goddess of love and fertility.

East–West Tensions

As the Persian Empire spread across the eastern Mediterranean in the sixth century B.C., Cyprus, along with other Greek islands, was annexed. In 499 B.C., it joined the Ionian Greek revolt but — after heroic resistance, notably during the prolonged siege of Paphos — was crushed by the Persian army the following year.

The Persians supported Phoenician expansion into the valuable inland copper belt. King Evagoras of Salamis countered by consolidating Greek power across the island, with backing from the Athenians. Artistic styles reflected the king's Hellenistic preferences but Persian motifs showed up in finely crafted jewelry, and in the architecture of massive fortifications.

From Alexander to the Caesars

In 333 B.C., Alexander the Great ended Persian supremacy in

the eastern Mediterranean and placed Cyprus under Macedonian rule. After his death in 323 B.C., his generals used the island as a battleground in the struggle over the succession, destroying many ancient cities in the process. By 299 B.C., Ptolemy I emerged the victor, and the city-kingdoms disap-

Ruins in Salamis recall the Hellenistic influence of King Evagoras.

peared as Cyprus became part of the Hellenistic state of Egypt. The Ptolemies ruled for 250 years until the Romans, on a pretext that the island was harboring pirates threatening their interests, annexed it to their province of Cilicia (the southern coast of modern Turkey).

In 48 B.C., Julius Caesar made a present of Cyprus to Cleopatra, the last member of the Ptolemaic dynasty. After her suicide, Augustus took it back for the Roman Empire and let his vassal, King Herod of Judaea, farm out the Cypriot copper concession to Jewish entrepreneurs.

The Byzantine Era

Despite the apostle Paul's mission to Cyprus in a.d. 45, the resolutely Hellenistic islanders continued in their attachment to the cults of Aphrodite and, with the growth of highly prized vineyards, the wine god Dionysos. Only in the fourth century, as Christianity took a hold on the Roman leadership, did churches and monasteries begin to spring up across Cyprus.

In A.D. 330, the Christian Empress of Byzantium, Helena, is said to have visited the island and founded the great Stavrovouni Monastery with a piece of the True Cross as its most cherished relic. Also around this time, the church won more friends when a special breed of cats were reared at St. Nicholas Monastery on the Akrotiri Peninsula in order to rid the island of a plague of snakes.

Priests wielded considerable power over everyday life, defending peasants against grasping tax collectors, but also demanding unquestioning allegiance. In 488, the archbishop of Cyprus gained undisputed control over the island's spiritual affairs and henceforth carried a scepter rather than a pastoral staff, and signed his name in imperial purple ink.

The Rise of Islam

With the Byzantine Empire weak from its war against Persia, the Arabs took the opportunity to cross over to Cyprus in 649 with a fleet of 1,500 ships. Salamis (now Constantia) was left in such ruins that it never recovered; the raid continued across the island until news of an approaching Byzantine fleet prompted retreat.

Four years later, in a move that foreshadowed events of the 20th century, the Arabs staged a second invasion and left a garrison of 12,000 men, encouraging Muslim immigration to establish a foothold. The Byzantines and the Muslim Caliphate subsequently agreed to neutralize Cyprus — there would be no military bases, though ports could be used for refitting the navy — and also to share tax revenues. Over the next 300 years, Muslims and Christians engaged in offshore battles and launched raids against each other, but also lived side by side.

The Crusades

During the Crusades, Cyprus became a key strategic post for Byzantine interests in Syria and Palestine. The governor organized protection for pilgrims to the Holy Land and supervised the rebuilding of Jerusalem's Holy Sepulchre and fortifications for its Christian Quarter. The invasion of Ottoman Turks in Anatolia and the Levant after 1071 threatened communications with Constantinople, but Cyprus was still able to supply food to soldiers in the First Crusade of 1097 and even provided refuge for defeated Muslim princes.

In the 12th century, the capital was moved to the safer inland location of Nicosia. New trade developed with Venice and the young Crusader states on the mainland. However, the

Turks' conquest of Anatolia in 1176 isolated Cyprus from the Byzantine government. Isaac Comnenius, a junior member of the imperial family, felt free to make himself the despotic "Emperor" of Cyprus, using Sicilian mercenaries to fight off the Byzantine fleet.

Salvation from his brutal cruelty seemed to come in the form of England's Richard the Lionheart, who docked at Limassol on his way to the Crusades. He crushed Isaac and was welcomed by cheering crowds in the streets of Nicosia.

Unfortunately the Cypriots soon realized Richard was not to be trusted. To pay for his expedition to the Holy Land, he stripped the island of all its money, and Greek Cypriots were denied any governing role. They were even ordered to shave off their beards, the supreme humiliation.

Lusignans, Genoese, and Venetians

After a tenure of a few months, Richard left the island in the hands of Guy de Lusignan, an ex-king of Jerusalem

Panayia Angelostikos, the 11th-century church near the village of Kiti, survives from the time of the Crusades.

A Stavrovouni monastery mosaic marks Christianity's rise in the Byzantine era.

from French Poitou. Lusignan brought in barons from war-torn Palestine with the promise of a safer life on Cyprus's fertile (and free) farm estates. The Lusignan dynasty's feudal rule reduced native Cypriots to serfdom. In 1260, the Roman Catholic Church was declared supreme on the island, though Orthodox priests maintained their status as the real spiritual authority inside the Greek-Cypriot community.

During the 14th century, Cyprus profited greatly as a Christian outpost, supplying the mainland crusaders. Famagusta's merchants in particular became renowned for their extravagant wealth. The island's opulence attracted pirates, and fueled a heated rivalry between the merchants of Genoa and Venice that erupted in bloody riots in 1345. The Cypriots sided with the Venetians against the Genoese, murdering merchants and looting shops in Famagusta. In retaliation, Genoa sent a fleet to ravage the whole island. In 1374, the Genoese extorted reparations of two million gold florins and confiscated the port of Famagusta.

By now, the Lusignan kings had become too decadent to resist Italian demands. James II needed help from the Sultan of Egypt to oust the Genoese in 1464, but the gold it cost him emptied his treasury. By various intrigues, the

Venetians stepped into the breach and ruled Cyprus for the next 82 years.

The Venetians' lucrative trade was threatened by Ottoman encroachment on three sides — Anatolia, the Levant, and Egypt. In 1570, the Turks demanded that Venice give up Cyprus. Imagining that attack would come from the east, the Venetians consolidated their defenses mainly in Famagusta. But the Turks landed on the south coast and headed inland to besiege the relatively lightly defended Nicosia, which fell after 46 days. The capital's Venetian commander was killed and his head sent to Captain Marcantonio Bragadino, the commander at Famagusta, as a warning. Undeterred, Bragadino led a heroic defense of the port city, with 8,000 Greek-Cypriot and Italian troops holding out for over 10 months against a Turkish army of 200,000. On 1 August 1571, with his ammunition gone, Bragadino surrendered. He was promised safe passage, but when the Turks saw that they had lost 50,000 men to such a tiny army, they were so enraged that they mutilated Bra-

The eyes have it — a startling depiction of the human form in a terracotta figurine detail from the fifth century B.C.

gadino and flayed him alive. Cyprus was now a province of the Ottoman Empire.

Turkish Rule

With the Turks controlling the whole of the eastern Mediterranean, Cyprus lost its strategic importance and was left to stagnate. Some 20,000 new settlers were brought in from Anatolia. The Turkish administrators proved more idle than oppressive and the island's infrastructure fell into ruin.

The only advantage for the Greek Cypriots was the regained status of the Orthodox Church. By 1660, the Sultan made their archbishop directly responsible for the Cypriot citizenry. He could and did appeal to the Sultan over the heads of local officials. This authority even extended to the collecting of taxes for the Ottoman treasury in order to counter the corrupt and often rebellious Turkish administrators.

During the Greek War of Independence of 1821, Archbishop Kyprianos let Greek rebel ships pick up supplies on the north coast. Turkey immediately sent in 4,000 Syrian troops. The archbishop and three of his bishops were executed. More troops were brought in from Egypt, resulting in large-scale massacres and the plunder of church property.

Royal Kykko Monastery is the place where Archbishop Makarios got his start.

Over the next 50 years, the Sultan tried to halt widespread abuses by Turkish tax collectors, which were provoking massive emigration of both Greek and Turkish Cypriots. But local Turkish officials opposed all reforms, often resorting to armed intimidation of governors sent in by the Sultan. The disintegration of Ottoman authority in Cyprus was symptomatic of the imminent collapse of the empire.

The British Step In

With "the sick man of Europe" on his deathbed, the superpowers of the time hovered around like vultures to pick at the remains, among which Cyprus was a choice little bone. Britain was concerned that the eastern Mediterranean remain safe for its ships to pass through the Suez Canal to India. To keep Russia out, Britain signed the Cyprus Convention with Turkey, whereby the island came under British administration while formally remaining the Sultan's possession. On 12 July 1878, the deal was sealed with a peaceful flag-raising ceremony in Nicosia.

The British envisaged the island less as a military base than as a staging area to assemble troops in case of joint action with Turkey in the Caucasus or — over a century before the Gulf War was to activate the plan — in Mesopotamia (modern Iraq).

The Green Line
The Green Line, which marks the division between north and south Cyprus, owes its name to the simple actions of a British army officer who drew a line in green ink on a map which approximated the de facto border. This subsequently became the official buffer zone. The Turkish name for the border is the Attila Line, after the code name Operation Attila for the 1974 invasion.

Greek Cypriots were happy about the transfer of power from corrupt Turks to upright Britons, and soon came to appreciate the new schools, hospitals, law courts, and roads that had become the hallmarks of British colonial administration. The population rose from 186,000 in 1881 to 310,000 in 1921. But the most important contribution they expected from the British would be to help Cyprus achieve *enosis*, or union with Greece, as Britain had done for the Ionian Islands in 1864. As long as he was in opposition, Gladstone supported the claim, but he did nothing about it when he became prime minister.

Union with Greece was, of course, opposed by the Turkish-Cypriot minority. They usually remained calm, confident that

A Small Nation's Great Leader

In Archbishop Makarios, Cyprus was blessed with a first president of powerful intellect and great spiritual authority. Born in 1913 to a poor peasant family in the Troodos Mountains, Mihail Christodoulous Mouskos became a monk at the Kykko Monastery. He studied at Athens and then in the United States, in Boston, from 1938 to 1948, when he returned to Cyprus to become Bishop of Kition (Larnaca).

Archbishop at the remarkably young age of 37, he won popular support with his dignified eloquence. But he was criticized by foreign observers for his failure to control Greek-Cypriot extremists, thus provoking alarm in the Turkish-Cypriot community. Nonetheless, he impressed the world with his moral leadership of non-aligned nations at the height of the Cold War, and his great physical courage during the Turkish invasion of 1974.

The Archbishop's original home in Panayia is open to visitors as is his tomb near Kykko Monastery (see page 74).

Britain would respect its alliance with Turkey and not give in to enosis demands. But violent demonstrations broke out when the Greek-Cypriot campaign grew vociferous.

In 1914, Turkey sided with Germany in World War I and Britain promptly annexed Cyprus, subsequently claiming it as a British Crown Colony. More roads were built, but little was accomplished in the direction of enosis. In 1931, impatient Greek-Cypriot members of the Legislative Council resigned, riots broke out in Nicosia, and Government House was burned down. Troops were brought in from Egypt. Insurgent bishops were deported, political parties banned, the Greek flag outlawed, and press censorship imposed. But during World War II, in response to the British alliance with Greece against Germany and Italy, Cypriots rallied to the British flag and furnished a 30,000-strong regiment. The island's political parties were duly reinstated.

Fight for Unity

In 1945, Britain thought it was doing Cyprus a favor by moving it toward self-rule. But the slogan of the day was "enosis and only enosis." In 1950 a plebiscite of Greek Cypriots voted 96 percent in favor of union with Greece, and the Church appointed a new leader, Archbishop Makarios III (see page 74).

In 1955, the campaign for enosis became an armed struggle led by Lieutenant-Colonel George Grivas, a Cypriot-born Greek Army officer. Directed from a hideout in the Troodos Mountains, EOKA (the Greek initials for the National Organization of Cypriot Struggle) blew up public buildings and killed opponents of enosis. Makarios publicly disowned the actions, but gave EOKA clandestine support. He was exiled in 1956, first to the Seychelles and then to Athens. The Greek public gave noisy support to the Greek-Cypriot cause, but their government was reticent.

Turkey backed the Turkish-Cypriot opposition to enosis with two main arguments: the Muslim community would be defenseless if swallowed up in the greater Greek nation; and Greek extension to Cyprus would pose a direct military threat to Turkey. In 1958, Turkish Cypriots rioted in favor of partitioning the island.

In 1959, Turks and Greeks met in Zurich, agreeing to renounce both enosis and partition, while guaranteeing strict safeguards to protect the Turkish-Cypriot minority. The president of the new independent republic would be Greek-Cypriot Archbishop Makarios, and his vice-president would be the Turkish-Cypriot leader, Fazil Kuchuk. On 16 August 1960, Cyprus became independent, though remaining within the British Commonwealth (with Britain retain-

Crowds gather at Nicosia's Orhodox cathedral, St. John's (Ayios Ioannis) — a survivor of the 18th century.

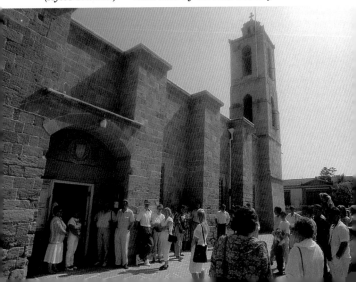

ing two military bases on the south coast). Grivas retired to Athens, unhappy with the outcome.

Troubled Independence

Cabinet posts, parliamentary seats, and civil service jobs were apportioned to Greek and Turkish Cypriots according to a fair ratio, and the main towns elected separate Greek- and Turkish-Cypriot municipal governments, but the constitution proved too complex to work.

In 1963, Makarios proposed 13 simplifying amendments that Turkey promptly vetoed, and fighting broke out in Nicosia. The British supervised a cease-fire and set up a "Green Line" (see page 30) separating the communities in the capital.

United Nations forces were brought in to patrol it in March 1964, and they have stayed ever since. Turkish-Cypriot enclaves were formed mainly in the northern part of the island and Turkey and Greece each sent in officers to train local forces.

In 1974, in a bid to regain popularity at home, Greece's military junta tried to impose *enosis* in Cyprus. Makarios resisted and demanded that the Greek officers be withdrawn from the island. The junta responded by engineering a military attack on the Presidential Palace in Nicosia. Makarios escaped to Paphos, where he broadcast to the people of Cyprus, refuting reports of his assassination.

This coup d'état gave Turkey a pretext to invade. Within three weeks, Turkish troops occupied most of northern Cyprus. Makarios escaped to New York, where he rallied support in the United Nations to reinstate him as president. He died in 1977. The Turkish army remained in control of 37 percent of the island, including Famagusta, northern Nicosia, and Kyrenia. Some 170,000 Greek Cypriots were forced to flee to the south, while about 30,000 Turkish Cypriots migrated to the north. By the early 1990s, approximately 80,000 new settlers had been brought into northern Cyprus from Turkish Anatolia.

In 1983, the so-called Turkish Republic of Northern Cyprus was set up under Rauf Denktash, but recognized only by Turkey, a situation that continues to this day. The UN Security Council condemned the move and urged the leaders to find a way other than partition to protect minority rights on the island. Because of the diplomatic isolation of the Turkish north, the economy in the region has stagnated badly. Greek Cypriots, on the other hand, have recovered well from the shock of invasion; today their economy is thriving again, thanks mainly to tourism.

Reunification with the north remains their goal but sadly shows no signs of becoming reality.

Bright light, big history: the old Paphos fort — at different times a Roman fort, a feudal castle, and a Turkish tower.

Historical Landmarks

ca 7000 B.C. First permanent settlements at Khirokitia and the Karpas peninsula.

ca 3500 B.C. Copper mines in Troodos foothills establish early wealth and strong export trade with Aegean and the Near East.

1200 B.C. Mycenaean Greeks settle and impart the island's Greek culture

700–350 B.C. Invasions by Assyrians and Persians.

333 B.C. Alexander the Great establishes Macedonian rule.

299-49 B.C. Cyprus joins the Hellenistic state of Egypt under the Ptolemy dynasty. Romans invade and add Cyrus to their empire.

a.d. 45 St. Paul's mission to Cyprus falls largely on deaf ears.

Fourth century Christianity takes hold; many churches built.

653 Arabs invade and garrison 12,000 men, Cyprus's original A.D. settlers.

1191–1192 Richard the Lionheart defeats the tyrant Isaac Comnenius and transfers the island to Guy de Lusignan, who builds a 300-year dynasty.

14th–15th centuries. Cyprus grows rich from supplying crusaders but is pillaged by Genoese. Venetians take over from Lusignans.

1571 Heroic fall of Famagusta to the Turks ends Venetian rule.

1571-1878 Turkish rule marked by neglect, stagnation, and mass emigration.

1878-1914 Cyprus comes under British administration, but possession is retained by Turkey. After Turkey sides with Germany in 1914, Britain annexes Cyprus.

1931 Enosis (unity with Greece) campaign builds force with riots.

1955 EOKA begins campaign of violence in pursuit of enosis.

1959–1964 Turkish and Greek Cypriots form joint administration that breaks down; leads to UN intervention along Green Line.

1974 Attempted coup by Greek military junta gives Turkey pretext to invade, occupying 37% of island, still held today.

1983 The "Turkish Republic of Northern Cyprus" is declared by the North, but recognized only by Turkey.

WHERE TO GO

If you really want to get to know Cyprus, rather than just soaking up the sun on its beaches, you should plan to stay in more than one place. And if your base is at one of the island's extremities — Paphos or Ayia Napa — it's a good idea to spend a night or so at a more central location such as Nicosia, Limassol, or Larnaca.

To help you plan your itinerary, we have divided the island into six sections:

Nicosia: The historic divided capital. Nearby are the ancient tombs of Tamassos, the monasteries of Ayios Herakleidos and Macheras, and the famous frescoes of Assinou Church.

Northern Cyprus: The starting point for this area is the checkpoint in Nicosia. Once across the border, there's the port of Famagusta and the ancient city of Salamis to the east, while Kyrenia, Bellapais abbey, and the breathtakingly situated castle of St. Hilarion lie to the north.

Larnaca & the East: The beaches of Ayia Napa and Protaras may be the focal points of the eastern part of the island, but the spectacular trip around Cape Greco is well worth the effort. To the west, near the resort (and port) of Larnaca, is the Hala Sultan Tekke mosque, the great Byzantine church of Kiti, Stavrovouni Monastery, and the handicraft village of Lefkara.

Limassol: Most hotels in Limassol are located east of this large cosmopolitan port city. There are some first-class historical sites nearby, however, including the old port with its fine castle museum, the crusader castle of Kolossi, and the splendid ancient Greek site of Kourion.

Troodos Mountains: If you are not staying overnight in the mountains, the most convenient base for this region is Limassol, within easy reach of the villages of Omodhos, Platres, and Kakopetria, and not far from Kykko monastery. But you can also explore the area from Paphos and Larnaca.

Paphos: This ancient capital and modern resort is the best all-round base on the island with its many historic attractions, beaches to the north, and Troodos mountain villages to the west. It is also well situated for exploring the beautiful, undeveloped Akamas Peninsula.

NICOSIA

Amid the animated prosperity of the town's southern sector, it is easy to forget the stretches of wall and barbed wire that make the divided capital a reluctant successor to Berlin.

Nicosia (*Lefkosia* in Greek, *Lefkosha* in Turkish) is Cyprus's only inland city. For tourists, everything of interest is handily confined within, or just outside, the old city walls. Most visitors just spend the day here, but if you also want to allot a full day for exploring Turkish-controlled northern Nicosia or Northern Cyprus, it's best to stay overnight. Be prepared for real heat. Nicosia is al-

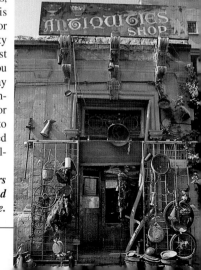

Northern Nicosia offers antiquities for sale and historic sites to explore.

ways around five degrees hotter than on the coast, with temperatures soaring above 30°C (86°F) in July and August.

Situated near the ancient site of Ledra, today's city was founded in the fourth century B.C. by Lefkon, son of Ptolemy I of Egypt. When the ancient coastal towns of Paphos and Salamis came under attack in the early seventh century A.D., the population shifted to the interior and Nicosia became the chief city. Under the Lusignans, it evolved into a splendid capital marked by elegant churches and monasteries in the French Gothic style.

Just prior to the Turkish invasion of 1570, the Venetians built the city's massive defensive wall. The city held out for seven weeks before the Ottoman Turks finally broke into the city and slaughtered 20,000 of its citizens. Resistance to Ottoman rule flared up into outright rebellion in 1821, but the Turks suppressed the revolt.

In a modern-day echo of those brutal times, the heaviest fighting of the 1974 Turkish invasion also took place around here. The eerie buffer zone with its burnt-out deserted buildings, UN checkpoints, rolls of barbed wire, sandbags, and roadblocks has become the city's most unwelcome tourist attraction. However, just a few yards away, you'll find a remarkably composed and buoyant city, virtually unrecognizable from any other prosperous town of its size in the Mediterranean.

> **Never refer to the Green Line as "the border" in front of a Greek Cypriot, as this implies that you recognize it officially as such. Call it "the buffer zone."**

The Fortifications

The ramparts hurriedly built by the Venetians remain Nicosia's dominant feature. Indeed, with its 11 pointed bastions and three giant gateways, the wheel-shaped Renaissance fortification has become the modern capital's distinctive logo.

The gates bear the names of the three coastal cities to which they lead: Famagusta to the east, Kyrenia to the north, and Paphos to the west (the two latter gates are in Turkish-Cypriot northern Nicosia).

Originally the main entrance to the old city, the massive tunnel-like **Famagusta Gate** has been restored as southern Nicosia's Cultural Center. Its stone barrel vaults provide a splendid setting for concerts, plays, and exhibitions of modern art, but they are only open to the public when an event is scheduled.

The sturdy Famagusta Gate, originally the main entrance to the city of Nicosia.

By contrast, the **Paphos Gate** is a small, unglamorous affair, surrounded by UN installations and the vestiges of war. Other bastions shelter municipal offices, while sections of the moat now serve as public gardens, playgrounds, and parking lots.

The Old City

Today, most visitors to the old city enter through **Eleftheria** (Liberty) **Square**, home to the Municipal Library, the Central Post Office, and the Town Hall. Off the square runs the old city's principal thoroughfare, **Ledra Street**. This pedestrian street is usually thronged with shoppers, even though it is a disappointingly modern and characterless strip.

Just off the southern end of Ledra Street, at 17 Hippocrates Street, is the award-winning **Leventis Municipal Museum**, which presents a beautifully designed account of Nicosia's history. Set in a fine 19th-century Neo-Classical mansion, exhibits include costumes, utensils, coins, and ancient ceramics.

Just behind the museum is the revived **Laiki Yitonia** (Popular Neighborhood) which purports to recreate the atmosphere of old Nicosia. Although it is actually a contrived tourist enclave, it's a very popular spot and by night is particularly pretty. Buildings in traditional style — some restored, others specially constructed — house quaint shops, tavernas, and artisans' galleries where you can watch craftsmen at work. There is an office of the Cyprus Tourism Organization here, from which walking tours (free of charge) depart on Monday, Tuesday, and Thursday at 10am.

Due north of Laiki Yitonia, walk along Aischylou Street to the minaret landmark of **Omerye Mosque,** transformed from the Augustinian monastery church of St. Mary's by the town's 16th-century Turkish conquerors. It is still used by the few hundred Moslem worshippers living in the Greek-Cypriot sector (mostly Arab students) and is open to visitors (don't forget to remove

The Phanoremeni Church: an eclectic and distinctive architectural mix.

your shoes). The minaret's spiral stairway is also open to visitors, but because the stairs tend to be messy near the top, you'll want to carry your shoes with you. From here, there are good views across to the northern sector and beyond to the Kyrenia Mountains.

Continue north on Solonos Street (on the back side of the minaret) to the landmark **Phanoremeni Church**. Although it only dates from 1872–1873 in its present form, it is a mix of several styles and features a fine iconostasis. Alongside it is a small squat ancient mosque, which is usually closed to the public. Head up Nikokleous Street to return to Ledra Street.

Ledra Street terminates at the **Buffer Zone,** where on a raised viewing point, manned by Greek-Cypriot soldiers, you can peer into the desolate no-man's land. The municipal tourist information office here is worth a visit if only to watch the 15-minute video on the history of the city. For even better views of "the other side," go to the observatory on the top floor of Woolworth's on Ledra Street.

Around the Archbishop's Palace

The **Archbishop's Palace** is a fanciful modern pastiche of Venetian-style architecture. Amid the splendor of the state rooms (closed to the public), Archbishop Makarios III installed an austere bedroom with a simple chest and an iron bed.

Housed in the public wing of the palace, the **Byzantine Museum** has rescued and restored a superb collection of icons from all over the island. Presented with loving care and attention to lighting, they offer the island's full range of Byzantine art, from a primitive ninth-century Virgin Mary to the decline of the genre in the 18th century. Don't miss an exhibition of 33 splendid mosaics that were dramatically recovered in the early and late 1990s after being stolen from Northern Cyprus.

Next to the museum, **Ayios Ioannis** (St. John's) is Nicosia's surprisingly small Orthodox cathedral, built in 1665 in an approximation of Late Gothic style. The colorful 18th-century frescoes, which completely cover the walls and ceiling, depict landmarks in the island's early Christian history.

The adjacent Gothic-arcaded monastery building is now the **Folk Art Museum**, displaying wooden water wheels, looms, pottery, carved and painted bridal chests, lace, and embroidered costumes. Opposite the nearby Pancyprian Gymnasium, a high school famous for its enosis activism in the 1950s, the **National Struggle Museum** documents the EOKA armed uprising against British rule in the 1950s. On display are a collection of weapons, old newspapers, and the command car of EOKA leader Griva Dighenis, a small burgundy-red Hillman.

Just south of the palace complex on Patriarch Grigorios Street is the house of Hadjigeorgakis Kornessios, better known as the **Konak Mansion**, a beautiful 18th-century structure with a Gothic-style doorway and overhanging, enclosed balcony. Restored to some of its original glory, the interior is notable for the ornate stairway and the grand reception room. They testify to the wealth accumulated by Kornessios, whose title *dragoman* signified that he was the official mediator between the Turkish sultan and Cypriot archbishop in the early 19th century.

☞ Cyprus Museum

The island's finest collection of antiquities is housed on Museum Street just south of the Green Line, near the Turkish-Cypriot sector's old Paphos Gate.

Exhibits of the Bronze Age include some of the first implements made from the island's all-important copper mines, red-polished and white-painted pottery. Look for the **sanctuary model** (2000 B.C.), in which worshippers and priests surround a bull sacrifice while a Peeping Tom on the sanctuary wall watches the secret ceremony.

An intriguing **Mycenaean krater** (drinking cup) imported to Enkomi by merchants from the Peloponnese in the 14th century B.C. has an octopus motif framing a scene of Zeus preparing warriors for battle at Troy. Nearby, a beautiful **blue faience rhyton** (ritual anointing vessel) from the 13th century B.C. depicts a lively bull-hunt in Kition.

Fascinating **royal tomb furniture** from Salamis (eighth century B.C.) includes an ivory throne, a bed, a sword, and the remains of two chariots and their horses' skeletons.

Perhaps the museum's most memorable highlight is the "Cyprus Terracotta Army," comprising around 1000 **votive statues and figurines** dating from between 625 and 500 B.C. Found at Ayia Irini in northwest Cyprus, the figurines are displayed just as they originally stood around an altar of an

The splendid Archbishop's Palace contains the superb
Byzantine Museum in its public wing.

open-air sanctuary. In a dual cult of war and fertility, soldiers, war chariots, priests with bull masks, sphinxes, Minotaurs, and bulls were fashioned in all sizes from life-size to just 10 cm (4 inches) tall, according to their ritual importance.

A true masterpiece of Roman-Cypriot art is the monumental bronze of **Emperor Septimius Severus** (c. A.D. 200). In contrast, behind the imperious emperor, is a touchingly child-like **Sleeping Eros**.

A new addition to the museum is a set of magnificent **Tamassos lions** from the royal tombs at Tamassos, found in 1997. Alongside is a double-sided limestone stele depicting Bacchus on one side and on the other, facing the wall, what is captioned an "erotic scene." Beware, if you have children in tow, it is indeed X-rated material! Mildly erotic too is the famous **Leda and Swan** mosaic taken from Palea Paphos (see pages 80–81).

Finally, look out for the gold pieces from the **Lambousa Treasure Hoard** and, in the last room, the small clay figures of women depicted while giving birth.

Northern Nicosia

Compared with the thriving southern half of the city, northern Nicosia is quiet and relatively impoverished. In fact, like much of the north, it has hardly moved on in tourist terms since 1974.

The sights here can be visited in a couple of hours or as part of a day trip to Northern Cyprus (see the box on page 37 for entrance requirements). From the checkpoint, walk along Sarai Onu Street to **Atatürk Square**, the hub of Turkish Nicosia. At its center is a granite column probably brought from Salamis by the Venetians.

From the square, head north along Girne Caddesi (Kyrenia Avenue) to the **Mevlevi Tekke**, once a ceremonial hall used by members of the whirling dervishes sect, who were outlawed in 1925. The 17th-century building with its several domes now houses a small **Ethnographic Museum** with

Visiting the North

The only way into Northern Cyprus for tourists staying in the south is through the checkpoint by the old Ledra Palace Hotel on Marcos Drakos Avenue in Nicosia. The crossing is open between 8am and 1pm to pedestrians only. It is an eerie experience to walk through the barbed wire blockades, rather like stepping into a 1960s Berlin spy film.

If you want to get in a full day's tour, arrive at the checkpoint by 8am, as you must return between 4:30 and 6pm. (You will be clearly informed of the exact return time when you cross.) Before crossing, with passport (which will not be stamped), you must check in with the Greek-Cypriot duty officer, then complete more paperwork on the Turkish side. Note too that you will probably only be allowed a maximum of two trips into the North for the duration of your stay in Cyprus.

Turkish-Cypriot taxis are waiting on the other side, though you can easily explore northern Nicosia on foot. It's a good idea to change at least a small amount of money into Turkish-Cypriot lira for the occasional drink or meal, but Greek-Cypriot money is accepted at museums and touristy restaurants, and a fair rate of exchange is usually given. Note that you are not allowed to bring Turkish souvenirs into the south. You can take photographs, but only of non-military or non-sensitive subjects. There is a heavy army presence in the north, so it is not a good idea to leave a video camera whirring. Finally, be aware that the border crossing may be closed at short notice (such as when groups of Greek Cypriots demonstrate nearby).

37

The Selimiye Mosque is a long-standing symbol of Nicosia's dual identity.

a reconstruction of the whirling dervishes' dance floor complete with mannequins (sadly static). The building itself is the star exhibit, but an arresting sight is the side room packed with the tombs of 16 Mevlevi sheiks, each set in perfect parallel formation to the next and identically covered in bright green cloths.

From Atatürk Square, Asmalti Street leads past a couple of old Turkish **khans** (inns) with picturesque courtyards and verandahs: Kumarcilar (Kumardjilar) Khan (open Monday–Friday) and the Büyük Khan (closed to visitors). Built in the 18th century by the Turks as hospices for visiting foreigners, they are rare survivors of their kind on the island.

A few meters farther east are the landmark minarets and lofty Gothic arches of the **Selimiye Mosque**, formerly the great Cathedral of St. Sophia, begun in 1209 and completed in the 14th century. Here the Lusignan princes were crowned kings of Cyprus, and Christian worship took place until the Turks turned the church into a mosque following the 1570 conquest.

Next door is the **Bedestan,** or old covered market, which dates from the 12th to the 14th centuries when it was constructed as the Church of St. Nicholas-of-the-English. The Turks converted the church into a covered market — today disused. But you can still admire the carved Gothic doors, the family crests and religious sculptures above the main portal, the barrel-shaped roof, its three apses, and dome. It now holds a Museum of Medieval Tombstones, though opening times are somewhat unpredictable.

Just behind the cathedral, the **Sultan's Library** preserves important books in Turkish, Arabic, and Persian, and is open to visitors.

Around Nicosia

The following excursions are all within 50 km (30 miles) of Nicosia, making them easy day trips.

Royal Tombs and Monasteries

The site of Tamassos, an ancient city-kingdom built on copper, is just over 12 km (7 miles) southwest of the capital, near the village of Politiko. Here excavations have uncovered a sanctuary and altar to Aphrodite, though the importance of this find is hard for the layperson to appreciate (it seems to be nothing but knee-high rubble). Of more general interest, however, are the site's two royal tombs (sixth century B.C.). Stairways descend to narrow *dromos*, passages carved in stone to imitate wooden dwellings, complete with simulated bolted doors, window sills, and "log-roof" ceilings. A set of magnificent stone lions and sphinxes from the site are on display at the Cyprus Museum (see page 34).

For a complete change in atmosphere, visit the nearby **Monastery of Ayios Herakleidos,** which is now in the hands of nuns who tend its gardens and sell honey, marzipan, and other sweets (closed daily 12–3pm mid-May to mid-September). After many restorations, the present

18th-century church houses, in a domed mausoleum, the remains of the saint who guided Paul and Barnabas on their mission to Cyprus. The first bishop of Tamassos, Herakleidos was burned alive by unbelievers; his skull and a hand bone were salvaged and are treasured in a bejeweled gold reliquary.

It's a short but difficult journey along unpaved roads to the **Monastery of Macheras**, 884 m (2,900 ft) up in the Troodos mountains. But once you are there, the views make it all worthwhile (note that visiting hours for tourists are limited to Monday, Tuesday, and Thursday 9am–noon). The monastery itself is a modern construction; an 1892 fire destroyed the original 12th-century foundation — although an allegedly miracle-working icon of the Virgin Mary survived. The region was a natural hideout for EOKA second-in-command Gregoris Afxentiou, who died in a battle with the British near the monastery in 1957. The site of his death (signposted) is now a place of pilgrimage for EOKA sympathizers.

Down the road beyond Gourri, the village of **Phikardou** represents a worthy effort to sustain Cypriot rural traditions. The whole village is protected as an Ancient Monument with a restoration program for its subtly colored ironstone houses and cobbled streets. The idea is not to create another folk museum, but to revitalize the community. Alas, it does not seem to be working. In 1992, when the scheme was in its infancy, there were just eight permanent residents. It was hoped that others might be enticed by the handsome reconstruction, but by 1999 the official population had actually declined to just seven! Wind your way past the church and the crumbling old buildings, scattering frightened lizards before you, and you will find side by side two museum houses: the **House of Katsinioros** and the **House of Achilles Dimitri** (open

Sunday–Monday 10:30am–2pm, Tuesday–Friday 9am–4pm, Saturday 9am–3:30pm). Here, accompanied by the museum keeper, you can see authentic old furnishings, a spinning wheel and loom, a winepress, and a brandy still.

Assinou Church

Stranded somewhat in the middle of nowhere, some 30 km (19 miles) west of Nicosia, is one of the gems of the Troodos foothills. Take the road past Peristerona, then follow the signs to the 12th-century hillside church of Assinou, which is famous for its magnificent Byzantine frescoes.

This modest but exquisite little church of ochre stone contains a veritable gallery of Byzantine art from the 12th to 16th centuries. But for a scene that is sublime beyond art, look back through the narthex to the frescoes framing the west door open to the green wooded slope beyond. The church is usually open, but if you find it closed, backtrack to the village of Nikitari to pick up the local priest who is the keeper of the key.

NORTHERN CYPRUS

The Turkish-occupied north, which comprises around 37 percent of the island, contains some of Cyprus's most beautiful natural regions, best beaches, most dramatic historical sites, and what

The Monastery of Macheras — well worth the difficult journey.

were once two of its finest towns. Ironically, the partition and political isolation have helped preserve the countryside from the ravages of mass tourism, particularly the beautiful golden sandy beaches of Famagusta, which remain undeveloped and mostly empty.

It is quite possible to whizz around the island in a day and cover all the main sights, but unless you are short on time, this is not recommended. In two day trips (one to the north, and one to the east) you can see all the sights in Northern Cyprus comfortably, including northern Nicosia (see page 36).

The Mountain Castles

The most striking of the Kyrenia Mountains is the Pentadaktylos (Five Fingers), whose stark silhouette inspired the writer Lawrence Durrell to give the mountains their second name, the Gothic range, in his travel memoir *Bitter Lemons*: "[it is] the *par excellence* Gothic range for it is studded with

St. Hilarion Castle offers a dizzying array of angles, towers, tiers, and, of course, views.

crusader castles pitched on the dizzy spines of the mountains, commanding the roads which run over the saddles between." Durrell lived on the northern slopes of the Kyrenia Mountains from 1953 to 1956.

Its fortresses lie now in noble ruin, victims not of enemy bombardment but of neglect by the Venetians, who could not afford their upkeep. Most spectacular of all is **St. Hilarion Castle**, which climbs and straggles along the knife-edge mountain ridges in three tiers of battlements and towers, finally reaching an altitude of around 670 m (2,200 ft) under twin mountain peaks. With steps continually leading both up and down to gate houses and wards, cisterns and barracks, royal apartments and stables, you may well feel as though you have stumbled into a baffling M. C. Escher drawing. Be prepared for a tiring climb if you are tackling all three levels, and think twice about attempting this in the sweltering midsummer heat.

The views are among the best in Cyprus. You can peer right down into the harbor of Kyrenia and, on a clear day, you can gaze some 100 km (60 miles) north to the mountains of Anatolia.

The castle was built around a church and monastery in the tenth century, honoring the hermit-saint Hilarion, who fled here when the Arabs advanced on Syria. The original Byzantine structure was fortified and extended by the Lusignans for their summer residence.

Kyrenia

Offering the most beautiful sheltered harbor in Cyprus and a grand old castle, this charming town — *Girne* in Turkish — is by far the best place to stop for lunch. The ancient buildings that line the harbor have more or less all been converted into bars or restaurants, but compared with the resorts on the south coast, it is a relaxed and understated place.

Overlooking the harbor is the massive bulk of **Kyrenia Castle,** which dates mostly from the 15th century. It has been used as a prison by each of the island's rulers, from the Byzantines to the British, the latter locking up EOKA fighters here in the 1950s. Today, the walls enclose a Byzantine chapel, royal apartments, and various historical displays. Most interesting of all, it serves as a museum for the **Kyrenia ship**, one of the oldest vessels ever recovered from the sea. This Greek trading ship sank off the coast of Cyprus about 300 B.C. and was discovered in 1965 by a sponge diver. The hull has been painstakingly reconstructed and is shown with part of its cargo.

☛ Bellapais Abbey

A short drive into the foothills behind Kyrenia leads to this superbly situated Gothic abbey. Looking down to the distant sea, it stands on a 30-m (100-ft) escarpment, its monastery buildings enclosing cypress trees, palms, and orange and olive trees. The abbey was originally built by the Lusignans for the Augustinian order. It took on its present form in the 13th century. The elegant arcade of the cloister is adorned with finely carved figures, while the vaulted refectory is a splendid space of six bays with a well-preserved rose window.

> **Don't discuss going to the north of the island in front of Greek Cypriots. They are not allowed to cross the Green Line, and for older folks, it may stir painful memories.**

☛ Famagusta

The east coast port of Famagusta was a mere village when Christian refugees arrived from Palestine in 1291. A century later, it had developed into a boom town of extravagant merchants and notorious courtesans where fortunes were

Kyrenia Harbor, the most attractive waterfront on the island, makes for a perfect lunch break.

won and lost overnight. For a brief time, it was one of the wealthiest cities in the world. All that ended in 1374 when the Genoese confiscated the port amid much bloodshed (see page 18). Worse was to come in 1571 with the invasion of the Turks and the most famous seige in the island's history (see page 19).

Famagusta rose again in this century to become the most important port in Cyprus and a major tourist center. But once again, in 1974, a Turkish invasion was to leave the city (renamed *Gazimagusa* in Turkish) a mere shadow of its former self. Since the departure of Greek Cypriots from the south, **Varosha**, the beach resort area, is eerily deserted and off-limits. Yet the Venetian fortifications and old town where Turkish Cypriots have always traditionally lived are still of great interest.

Highlights

Byzantine Museum, Nicosia. The best collection of icons in Cyprus. (See page 33.)

Cyprus Museum, Nicosia. The island's finest collection of antiquities. (See page 34.)

Assinou Church, Troodos Mountains. Tiny 12th-century church with exquisite Byzantine frescoes in a glorious wooded setting. (See page 41.)

St. Hilarion Castle, Northern Cyprus. Breathtakingly situated Crusader castle with fabulous views. (See page 43.)

Kyrenia The most beautiful harbor in all of Cyprus, ideal for lunch. (See page 43.)

Stavrovouni Monastery, west of Larnaca. Magnificent views, but sadly, off-limits to women. (See page 54.)

Monastery of Ayia Napa Beautiful Venetian architecture and serene Gothic cloister. (See page 56.)

Nissi Beach, Ayia Napa. The softest sand on the island, deluged by bodies in summer, but in the off-season, a picture-postcard delight. (See page 57.)

Cape Greco viewpoint Breathtaking cliff top views of sea and land with the occasional bonus of hang gliders. (See page 57.)

Konnos Bay Fringed by pine trees, dotted by yachts at anchor, and set away from the main resorts, this is surely the loveliest sandy beach cove in Cyprus. (See page 58.)

Kourion Cyprus's archaeological highlight with a wonderful cliff-top setting. Occasional performances at theater. (See page 63.)

Aphrodite's Birthplace It's easy to scoff at the legend, but one look at this beautiful rocky bathing place and you'll soon have your swimsuit on. (See page 67.)

Paphos Mosaics More than just decorative floors, these remarkable survivors are works of ancient art. (See page 77.)

Tombs of the Kings Feel a bit of Egypt and a hint of Petra in this intriguing and atmospheric city of the dead. (See page 78.)

Akamas Peninsula The last great wilderness of southern Cyprus — best explored off road, but if short on time, visit the beautiful rocky coves by the Baths of Aphrodite. (See page 83 .)

By the harbor stands the Citadel, better known as the **Tower of Othello**, which is associated with a 16th-century Lieutenant-Governor of Cyprus named Christoforo Moro, who is sometimes cited as the model for Shakespeare's tormented Moor. Most formidable of the Venetian fortifications is the **Martinengo Bastion** in the northwest corner of the old town. Its walls, 4–6 m (13–19 ft), proved a painful thorn in the side of the Turks during the siege of 1570.

It was the Lusignans who built the town's churches, at one time said to number 365. The finest of these was St. Nicholas Cathedral, which was converted with one slim minaret to become the **Lala Mustafa Pasha Mosque**, named after the commander of the Turkish invasion of 1570. This handsome French-Gothic structure was completed in 1326 with a majestic western façade worthy of any of the great European cathedrals. Although as a mosque the interior has been stripped of human representation in sculpture or fresco — and damaged by earthquake in 1735 — it can still be admired for its pristine Gothic features.

Salamis

Directly overlooking the sea just 8 km (5 miles) north of Famagusta, this ancient city-kingdom is on a par with Kourion (see page 63) as the finest archaeological site on the island. It may lack Kourion's dramatic cliff-top setting, but makes up for it with a splendid sandy beach right by the ruins.

For 2,000 years, Salamis was the leading city in Cyprus and a favorite haven for Greek artists and intellectuals exiled from Athens. As Constantia, it became capital of early-Christian Cyprus in A.D. 395, subsequently suffering from earthquake destruction and disappearing completely after the Arab invasion of 647.

The anicent Roman theater recalls a time when Salamis was the most important city in Cyprus.

Visible ruins today date from Hellenistic, Roman, and Byzantine times. The **Roman theater** probably succeeded an earlier Greek structure and its 50-row auditorium seated 15,000 — the largest in Cyprus. Also most impressive is the spacious **gymnasium** (high school). The graceful Corinthian columns were brought here from the theater and re-erected by the Byzantines. In the adjoining **public baths**, you can distinguish the *frigidarium, tepidarium,* and the *caldarium.* The water was channeled from Kythrea, 60 km (37 miles) away via a Roman aqueduct that still stands.

A couple of minutes' drive west of Salamis is the **Mausoleum of St. Barnabas**, who was the fellow apostle of Paul on their mission to Cyprus in A.D. 45. (He was martyred in Salamis at the hands of Jews he was trying to convert.) The rock-cut burial chamber is now empty, but its discovery some 400 years later helped the Church of Cyprus achieve autonomy within the Orthodox faith, and led to the building of the monastery nearby. The present drum-domed church was built in 1756 with elements from an earlier 15th-century church and columns and capitals from Salamis. It is now a museum of Byzantine icons, though sadly, its best examples have been looted.

LARNACA AND THE EAST

Larnaca has benefited considerably from the 1974 partition. Its airport has replaced Nicosia's as Cyprus's international port of entry, the population has almost doubled since the influx of refugees (mostly from Famagusta) that followed the 1974 partition, and the seaport is reviving. Beach resort facilities have also burgeoned.

Much of northern Larnaca is built over the ancient city-kingdom of Kition. Legend attributes its founding to Kittim, a grandson of Noah. Excavated traces of dwellings from the second millennium B.C. make this the oldest continuously inhabited city in Cyprus. Phoenicians prospered from the export of copper from Tamassos, and many centuries later, Lusignan barons revived the town as an important commercial and shipping center. Under the Turks, the foreign merchants who made it their home and the many consulates needed to protect their interests gave the town a cosmopolitan air.

The Seafront

The attractive palm-tree lined Foinikoudes (Palm Tree) Promenade is home to hotels, international restaurants, cafés, and fast-food joints. At the north end is the pleasure-boat marina. A classical bust of the heroic Athenian General, Kimon, who led the fleet to recapture Kition from the Persians in 450 B.C. (but died in the attempt), reminds visitors of the area's ancient past.

From the marina, the dark, compacted, sandy town beach stretches almost to the old fort that marks the heart of what was the Turkish quarter. **Larnaca fort**, built by the Turks in

1625, now contains a small museum of archaeological finds from Kition and Hala Sultan Tekke (see page 52). From the ramparts, there are good views of the harbor.

Across the street is the **Djami Kebir Mosque** (founded in the late 16th century), now a peaceful haven that serves Arab students and businessmen. Notice the tombstones with turbans in the little corner graveyard, a rare sight so close to a mosque.

☞ Church of St. Lazarus

A couple of blocks inland from the mosque (at the end of Dionysou Street), is the three-tiered campanile of the town's most revered church, dedicated to the man Jesus raised from the dead. According to legend, the locals of his hometown, Bethany, were not much impressed by this miracle, and Lazarus was expelled in a not particularly seaworthy boat that nevertheless got him as far as Kition. Here, where he was better appreciated, Lazarus settled, became bishop, and died (this time for good!). The church erected over his tomb has been rebuilt many times. Its present style is an eclectic mixture of extravagant Byzantine, Romanesque, and Gothic styles with a fine iconostasis. The remains of Lazarus were removed from here in 890 and brought to Constantinople. In the crypt below the iconostasis, you can see the empty, though still much venerated, sarcophagus.

> **Men should always wear long trousers and women should always wear a long skirt when visiting monasteries.**

Larnaca Museums

Just opposite the marina, housed in old Customs warehouses, are the **Municipal Art Gallery** and the **Pierides Paleontological Museum**, both opened in 1999. They are

"Built by angels" — the interior of the Panayia Angelostikos, which houses a fine Byzantine mosaic in its apse.

worth a quick look if only to view their temporary exhibitions. One block inland is the tourist office from where walking tours of Larnaca depart each Wednesday and Friday at 10am.

Diagonally across from the tourist office, on Zeno Kitieos Street, is the town's finest collection, the **Pierides Museum**. Situated in an old family home which provides a charming setting, you'll find hundreds of archaeological finds and works of art, tracing Cypriot history from Neolithic to Byzantine times.

Highlights include pottery of carved stone and red-polished clay; expressive statuettes; idols of Astarte (the Phoenician counterpart to Aphrodite); medieval glazed ceramics; Roman glassware; and Cypriot embroidery, costumes, and furniture. Next to the museum is a sculpture garden containing several amusing and clever avant-garde pieces.

The **Larnaca District Archaeological Museum** is a ten-minute walk northwest of the city center, at the corner of Kilkis and Kimon streets. Of principal interest here are the prehistoric finds from the nearby sites of Khirokitia (see page 54), Kalavassos, and Kition (see page 52).

Uphill, just beyond the District Museum, the **Kition Acropolis,** dating from the 13th century B.C., will probably only appeal to seasoned archaeology buffs.

West of Larnaca

About 5 km (3 miles) from town, in the direction of the airport, lies the Salt Lake that once provided a source of valuable income to ancient Larnaca. Lying 3 m (10 ft) below sea level, it is a true lake only in spring; each year at the end of July, the salt is collected after the lake dries up. In autumn and winter, thousands of migratory flamingoes pass through in a colorful cloud of pink.

The **Hala Sultan Tekke**, a Muslim mosque-cum-monastery, looks like a mirage in the dry summer season, thrusting its minaret through greenery and palm trees over the blinding salt flats. The shrine contains the remains of the Prophet Mohammed's maternal aunt and foster mother, Umm

Icons in the lower chapel of Stavrovouni Monastery, founded by the Empress Helena in A.D. 330.

Haram ("Sacred Mother"), known as Hala Sultan in Turkish, and is consequently Cyprus's most important place of Muslim pilgrimage. According to Muslim tradition, Umm Haram came to Cyprus with a party of Arab invaders in 647. Unfortunately she fell from her mule near the Salt Lake, broke her neck, and was buried here. The Turks built the mosque in her honor in 1816.

The outer room has brightly painted octagonal columns and there is a gallery for women to the right. In the inner sanctuary, the guardian (who also acts as a guide) will point out the trilithon structure above Umm Haram's grave — two enormous stones about 4.5 m (15 ft) high, covered with a meteorite that is said to have come from Mecca and to have hovered in the air by itself here for centuries.

Some 8 km (5 miles) farther west is the village of Kiti and its famous church **Panayia Angelostikos**, which literally translates as "built by angels." Domed and in golden stone, the present 11th-century edifice replaces a much earlier structure. Its outstanding feature is a splendid early Byzantine **mosaic** in the apse, considered to be among the finest in Cyprus. The standing Virgin Mary holds the Christ Child, flanked by the archangels Michael and Gabriel.

At an altitude of about 730 m (2,400 ft), Lefkara — 50 km (30 miles) from Larnaca — is actually two villages, **Pano Lefkara** and **Kato Lefkara**, which occupy a picturesque site in the foothills of the Troodos mountains. The name Lefkara is synonymous with drawn embroidery (*lefkaritika*), the traditional cottage industry that has brought the village fame for over five centuries. Widely but incorrectly termed as lacework, lefkaritika is actually linen openwork, stitched with intricate geometric patterns.

Women still work in narrow streets and courtyards, patiently turning out embroidered articles which you can buy from them or in one of the many shops. A few years ago there were less than a dozen outlets, today there are over 50 — which would be more than enough in a city the size of Larnaca. As a result, hustling, albeit of the mild kind, is common practice. However, you don't even need to come to Lefkara any more to buy lefkaritika, as it is now available all over Cyprus. The other specialty of the village shops is silver.

Smaller and overlooked by the masses is Kato Lefkara. With many of its traditional houses recently restored and window and door frames painted in bright Mediterranean blue it's a very pretty place.

A few kilometers south, archaeologically-inclined visitors may like to make a detour to **Khirokitia**, a small village known for its neolithic ruins. One of the oldest sites in Cyprus, it dates back to 7000 B.C. The most interesting of the four areas is the main street with its stone foundations of bee-hive-shaped houses called *tholos*. The village's most interesting artifacts are exhibited in Nicosia's Cyprus Museum.

On the way back to Larnaca, make a detour to the famous hill-top monastery of **Stavrovouni** (Mountain of the Cross), which sits just off the road to Nicosia. At an altitude of 689 m (2,260 ft), it affords an unbeatable view north across Nicosia and the plain to the blue Kyrenia mountains beyond, and south over neatly terraced hills to the Salt Lake, Larnaca, and the Mediterranean. Stavrovouni is built on the site of a shrine to Aphrodite which, like the monastery today, was off-limits to women. Nevertheless, Helena, mother of Emperor Constantine, is said to have ventured up here to found the monastery with a piece of the True Cross in A.D. 330 (see page 15). This relic is still proudly displayed in the monastery church. Note that cameras are strictly forbidden anywhere inside

Picturesque Nissi Beach is best enjoyed out of season, when it's free of holiday throngs.

the grounds — so you will only be able to record that magnificent view in your head.

At the foot of the long and winding road that ascends up to Stavrovouni is the **Monastery of Ayia Varvara** (St. Barbara), which is open to visitors in the morning and late afternoon (closed noon–3pm). Of more interest is the **Studio of Father Kallinikos** just across the road. This elderly white-bearded monk is a star of Cyprus Tourism travel posters, pictured doing what he does best, painting icons. Father Kallinikos is a world-renowned expert in his field and it is fascinating to watch him at work in his small, rather ramshackle studio, where some of his works are for sale.

East of Larnaca

The island's southeast corner is not only a major resort area, but also its vegetable garden. Potatoes, eggplants, tomatoes, cucumbers, and onions are all-important produce for export, grown in the fertile red soil of the local villages. But here, too, the politico-military realities of Cyprus become apparent. Just beyond the Larnaca Bay resort hotels, you pass through the British Sovereign Base Area of **Dhekelia**. The Greek-Cypriot republic is squeezed here into a narrow strip by the border of the Turkish-occupied zone, which swoops south to include Famagusta. Immediately east of Dhekelia is **Potamos**, a picturesque fishing creek flanked by a couple of good tavernas.

Following the Turkish occupation of Famagusta, **Ayia Napa** has been transformed from a tiny fishing village into Cyprus's major party resort. As you enter the town, its character is evident from the large number of international bars and restaurants and cheap seaside souvenir shops, but the change is most pronounced in the square around the venerable **Monastery of Ayia Napa** (Our Lady of the Forest). Today, aside from one ancient sycamore said to be 600 years old, the only forest is that of concrete pillars and neon signs which mark the island's largest and tackiest concentration of bars and nightspots.

Still, if you visit during the day (when most of Ayia Napa's party animals are either asleep or at the beach), the square is completely quiet and the monastery is peace personified. Built around 1530, originally as a nunnery, it remains one of the island's most handsome surviving Venetian buildings. Seek out a moment of tranquillity in its Gothic

The Dead Zone

The most intriguing of the many boat trips out of Ayia Napa and Protaras is one that goes as far as Famagusta to view the decaying holiday town of Varosha. Once a major 4000-bed resort, it has been left to rot since 1974 when it was declared UN territory (even though it is policed by the Turkish army). Varosha may also be viewed from a couple of cafés in Dherinia using the binoculars provided for a small fee.

cloister and courtyard that features a charming octagonal marble fountain. Carved out of the rock, the church lies partially underground. The monastery is now a conference center for the World Council of Churches, and its church is only open regularly for Sunday services.

The only other cultural attraction of note is the **Marine Life Museum**, a 5- to 10-minute walk uphill behind the monastery. It contains a number of shells, fossils, and taxidermic marine specimens.

Ayia Napa's growth is largely a result of its splendid beaches of fine golden sand, a rarity in Cyprus. The main strand is **Nissi Beach**, a picture-postcard sandy strip and cove with limpid blue waters and a tiny island (*nissi* in Greek) within paddling distance. It's a lovely place to come out of season, but in midsummer it becomes horribly crowded. To compound the mayhem, there's also bungee-jumping here.

Nearby at **Makronissos**, another popular sandy beach, are 19 rock tombs which date from the Classical and Hellenistic periods.

Around Cape Greco

For anyone over the age of 30 who can't quite see the point of Ayia Napa, there's the island's southeastern tip, Cape Greco, whose spectacular rocky coves, caves, and bays provide an escape from the crowds.

Head west on the E360 toward the Cape and just outside the town, by the Grecian Bay Hotel, are the **Thalassines Spilies** sea caves, famous for a much-photographed sea arch and frequented by snorkelers and divers. A few kilometers farther along the main road are the more spectacular **Palatia** (Palace) **caves**.

Continue along the same road and turn off at the **Cape Greco viewpoint**. You will have to leave your car and walk

All grapes, no wrath — while in Limassol, take the opportunity to tour a winery.

the last 500 m (1500 ft) uphill, but it is well worth the effort. Perched high at an altitude of almost 100 m (300 ft), the view looking back west is stupendous, and benches have been thoughtfully provided for those who prefer to sit while taking it all in. Immediately to the east is **Cape Greco** itself, the easternmost point of the island. The point is occupied by Radio Monte Carlo and is off-limits to visitors.

Heading north will bring you to **Konnos Bay**, probably the most picturesque sandy beach cove in all of Cyprus. On a quiet day, it can be heaven. In midsummer, Ayia Napa "booze cruises" with booming sound systems destroy the peace.

The same coast road continues north to the lovely sandy beaches of Fig Tree Bay around which the characterless resort of **Protaras** has sprung up. There are no signs to the beaches, but just look for the big hotels. All water sports are practiced here.

LIMASSOL

Limassol is Cyprus's indigenous good-time town, with plush restaurants and a brash and boisterous nightlife. Fittingly, it plays host to the island's wildest pre-Lenten Carnival. However, most visitors see relatively little of the city itself, as accommodation is well away from the center in a strip of high-rises some 10–15 km (6 1/4–9 1/2 miles) east.

It was here that England's Richard the Lionheart, leading a Crusade to Jerusalem in 1191, stopped off with his fiancée Berengaria. Refused provisions by the tyrant Isaac Comnenius, Richard responded by defeating him in battle, then selling Cyprus — first to the Knights Templar (who settled in Limassol), and then to the Lusignans (see pages 17–18). The crusader Knights of St. John settled in Limassol in 1291 and the town flourished as never before.

But by the early 19th century, earthquakes and the rapacity of the Genoese and the Turks had reduced the city to a crumbling village. Development of the wine industry under the British breathed new life into the place.

Since the 1974 partition, Limassol's population has increased by 50 percent to more than 150,000, second only to that of Nicosia. Besides refugees from the north, it counts a notable community of Lebanese, prosperous immigrants from the Near East, and a burgeoning number of Russian businessmen.

Inside the City

The solitary surviving monument to the town's feudal glory is **Limassol Castle**, whose solid imposing stone fortification dates from the 13th century. Today it houses the **Cyprus Medieval Museum**, one of the island's best collections, with some particularly well preserved ancient tombstones, and suits of armor that reflect the local metal-working tradition. The building itself is as interesting as its exhibits. Get up on top of the roof for fine views over this part of town.

The area around the castle is particularly pleasant with tropical greenery in its gardens and a clutch of pretty pavement cafés and historic buildings. The narrow lanes around here used to comprise the Turkish commercial

Major Museums

Cyprus has many museums that showcase the island's diverse art history. Here are the most important:

Leventis Municipal Museum *17 Hippocrates Street, Nicosia; Tel. (02) 451475.* Colorful account of Nicosia's checkered history. Open Tue–Sun 10am–4:30pm. Free. (See page 32.)

Byzantine Museum/Archbishop's Palace *Nicosia; Tel. (02) 430008.* Wonderful collection of icons and mosaics. Open Mon–Fri 9am–4:30pm, Sat 9am–1pm. C£1. (See page 34.)

Konak Mansion/House of Hadjigeorgakis Kornessios *Patriarch Grigorios Street, Nicosia; Tel. (02) 305316.* Fascinating look inside the 18th-century house of a dragoman. Open Mon–Fri 8am–2pm, Sat 9am–1pm. 75c. (See page 34.)

Cyprus Museum *1 Museum Street, Nicosia; Tel. (02) 865864.* The very best of Cyprus's rich archaeological heritage. Open Mon–Sat 9am–5pm, Sun 10am–1pm. C£1.50. (See page 34.)

Pierides Museum *Zinonos Kitieos Street, Larnaca; Tel. (04) 652495.* Charmingly old-fashioned museum of archaeology and works of art. Open summer Mon–Fri 9am–1pm, 4–7pm; winter Mon–Fri 9am–1pm, 3–6pm. C£1. (See page 51.)

Cyprus Medieval Museum *Limassol Castle, near old port; tel (05) 330419.* Fascinating medieval exhibits, but the star is the castle building. Open Mon–Sat 9am–5pm, Sun 10am–1pm. C£1. (See page 59.)

Kourion Archaeological Museum *Episkopi; no Tel. number.* Essential viewing before a visit to the marvelous site of Kourion. Open Mon–Fri 9am–2:30pm. 75c. (See page 63.)

Paphos District Archaological Museum *Griva Dighenis Avenue (Limassol Road), Paphos; Tel. (06) 240215.* The best collection of antiquities outside Nicosia. Open Mon–Sat 9am–5pm, Sun 10am–1pm. 75c. (See page 80.)

quarter. You may enter the mosque which lies a few meters from the castle and is still used by Limmasol's sizeable Arab population. Behind it, you can peer into excavations of an even older mosque. For the particularly adventurous (or particularly grubby), there's a working Turkish bath (*hamam*) nearby.

As you wander around this interesting quarter, you will see artisans' workshops, often quite primitive, where the specialty is metalware (particularly copper and tin).

It is just 1 km (^{1}/2 mile) along the seafront promenade from the old port to the **municipal gardens**, a pleasant place to rest for a while. There's also a miniature "zoo" that contains mostly birds. If you are walking from the old port, go via Ayios Andreas Street to see the Folk Art Museum en route (see below).

At the far end of the gardens, the small, modern **Limassol District Archaeological Museum** contains some fascinating archaeological treasures. Don't miss the display of jewelry and the expressive terracotta figurines. There's a beautiful head of Aphrodite from nearby Kourion and a massive statue of the ugly Egyptian god Bes from the site of ancient Amathus.

From the gardens, it's a 5-minute walk (back toward the port) along Giagkou Tornariti Street to the **Folk Art Museum**, which provides a glimpse of rural Cypriot life through wood-carving, embroidery, jewelry, and weaving.

Wine-making is not only an industry but also a tourist attraction, so you'll find a visit to a **winery** both instructive and enjoyable. The top houses — Keo, Sodap, and Etko — cluster together on Franklin Rooseveldt Boulevard (a 5- to 10-minute walk west of the castle). All offer short tours which usually begin around 9:30 or 10am and always end with a tasting.

East of Limassol

East of town, hidden among the beach resort hotels, are the fenced-off ruins of the agora of **Amathus**, one of the island's oldest city-kingdoms. It is really only of interest to archaeological experts, though there is a good brief explanation on a board at the site.

A few kilometers farther on is **Governor's Beach** (a local bus connects with all major hotels), a dark-sand beach which is largely uncommercial and, weekends aside, usually quiet.

Akrotiri Peninsula

It was here that the traces of the earliest human presence on the island — pigmy hippo hunters — were found (8500 B.C.). Half of the peninsula is salt lake — more flats than lake — popular with migratory birds, notably pink flamingoes, from October to March. Most of the remainder of the peninsula is occupied by the British Sovereign Base Area.

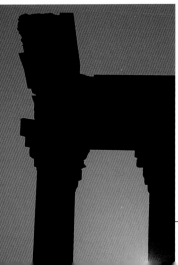

Just south of **Akrotiri** village, a bumpy track leads east to **St. Nicholas of the Cats Monastery**. The fame of the monastery has everything to do with the special breed of anti-viper cats its monks reared (see page 15); today's institution is a mod-

Stone ruins for the woodland god — find peace in the Sanctuary of Apollo Hylates.

ern building with little of historical or architectural interest, run by four nuns.

To the north of the peninsula, the impressive 15th-century keep of **Kolossi Castle** is one of the icons of Cypriot tourism. It was the headquarters of the Knights of St. John; from here, they administered their considerable sugar plantations and vineyards. The *Commanderie,* as the headquarters was known, gave its name to their prized Commandaria dessert wine, which is still produced today (see page 90).

Among the spacious rooms, all now empty, the one with a huge walk-in fireplace was the kitchen. In the adjacent room is a damaged fresco, the only decoration that has survived in the castle. Climb the steep and narrow spiral staircase for the view from the battlements. Outside you can see traces of an ancient aqueduct, while the imposing stone Gothic structure across from the keep served as the knights' sugar refinery.

Kourion

Before exploring the great archaeological site of Kourion, stop off in the nearby village of Episkopi to do a little homework at the **Kourion Museum**, which also holds dramatic recent finds from the earthquake that devastated Kourion in A.D. 365. On display is a touching group of three human skeletons, a 25-year-old male protecting a 19-year-old female with an 18-month-old baby clutched to her breast. Among the more conventional exhibits are a Roman stone lion fountain, terracotta vases, and figurines.

Kourion itself lies just west of Episkopi, and along with Salamis in Northern Cyprus (see page 47), is the most important archaeological site on the island. Not the least of its attractions is its spectacular setting high on a bluff above

Episkopi Bay. In ancient times, sacrilegious criminals were hurled to their death on the rocks below. These days, daredevil sportsmen hurl themselves toward the rocks below — but with a hang glider firmly attached to their backs.

Current historical opinion attributes the town's foundation to Mycenaean settlers in the 13th century B.C. Known as Curium to the Romans, it converted to Christianity in the fourth century A.D., with its faith sorely tested by a devastating earthquake in 365. After Arab raids in the seventh century, the bishopric moved out to what is now Episkopi, leaving Kourion to sink into oblivion.

The site is large. Drive past the gatehouse before you start to explore on foot. Your first stop is in front of the extensive ruins of the city, which include the *agora* (marketplace) and *nymphaeum* (fountain house). Unfortunately, this area is fenced off to visitors as long-term excavations continue. Turn to the left to roam through the remains of the **early Christian cathedral**. The plan of this basilica reveals 12 pairs of granite columns for the nave. To the left (north) is the baptistery where, in a dressing room, people disrobed and were anointed with oil before descending to the cross-shaped font.

Siga siga —
Slowly, slowly!
(Take your time)

Opposite the cathedral are the fenced-in ruins of a colonnaded portico paved with what is known as the **Achilles mosaic** (fourth century A.D.). It depicts Achilles, disguised as a woman to avoid enlistment in the Greek expedition, tricked by Odysseus into grabbing a spear and shield and revealing his true identity. The nearby **House of the Gladiators** is so named for its fine mosaics of two duels, one with a very aristocratic-looking referee — perhaps the owner of the house. Return to your car and drive on to the reconstructed **Roman theater** built between A.D. 50 and 175. It

Despite its fame, Aphrodite's Birthplace has remained largely uncommercialized and is a good place for a dip.

occupies a spectacular sloping site on the edge of the bluff. The amphitheater once seated 3,500 and is used today for a variety of open-air performances (see page 92). At the end of the second century A.D., the theater spiced up its shows by pitting man against beast.

Behind the theatre is the Roman **Villa of Eustolios**. The welcoming mosaics of birds and fish indicate that Eustolios was a man of wealth and taste; inscriptions to both Apollo and Jesus Christ suggest that, at least from a religious perspective, he was prudent enough to hedge his bets. Eustolios later added on a public bathhouse. The central room features some more remarkable mosaics, including one of a partridge and another of Ktisis, a deity who personifies creation. She holds what looks like a 12-inch ruler, a symbol of her function.

Watch the water fall: the Troodos region is full of spectacular cascades.

On the main road about 1 km (1/2 mile) west of the main site are the scant remains of the **stadium** where athletics were performed on a U-shaped track before some 6,000 spectators. On the opposite side of the road, there's a stopping place for a wonderful view down to **Curium Beach.**

Continue west to the **Sanctuary of Apollo Hylates** (God of the Woodland). Apollo was worshipped here from the eighth century B.C., but most of the present structures were put up around A.D. 100, then toppled by the great earthquake of 365. From the guardian's lodge, take the path west to the pilgrims' entrance (through the stumpy remains of the Paphos Gate). The buildings here were probably hostels and storehouses for worshippers' votive offerings. The surplus was carefully placed in the *vothros* pit (at the center of the site), which was full of terracotta figurines, mostly horse riders — still intact when uncovered by the archaeologists. Follow the path along the sanctuary's main street to the Temple of Apollo. It has been partially reconstructed to appear as it did in A.D. 100, with simplified Corinthian capitals on its columns. Today, thanks to the posters of the Cyprus Tourism Organization, it has become the most photographed symbol of the island's antiquity.

West to Aphrodite's Birthplace

If the flat, hard-packed sands of Curium Beach don't attract you, try the coarse sand and shingle of Avdimou Beach, a little farther west. But if you crave the creature comforts of a resort (albeit a fledgling resort), then continue on to **Pissouri**. Note that the signs to both Avdimou and Pissouri are to the inland villages; follow the signs for Avdimou Beach or Pissouri Bay, which changes to "K. Pissouri" (short for Kato, or Lower Pissouri), then finally to "Pissouri Jetty." The latter is a pretty little sheltered place, also with a coarse sand-and-shingle beach.

It is easy to be skeptical about a few rocks in the sea which claim to be the birthplace of a goddess, let alone the island's most famous deity, but this stretch of coastline and the **Petra tou Romiou** rock formation, better known as **Aphrodite's Birthplace**, is undoubtedly a beautiful natural sight. Curiously, its name, which translates as Rock of Romios, has nothing to do with Aphrodite, but commemorates the Byzantine hero Romios. He must also have been endowed with supernatural powers, as he is said to have used the rocks as missiles to ward off pirates. The views east, away from the rock to the blinding white sea cliffs, are also spectacular. The most popular vantage point is opposite the rocks, where there is a parking area and café. But if you don't want to risk prematurely joining the gods, do *not* race across the dangerously busy road at this point (as so many people do). Cross via the underpass next to the café.

> **Sign on departing villages and towns:**
> *Kalo taxidhi* — **Bon Voyage**

The water is clear and inviting and, as it's not every day you get the chance to swim in a god's birthplace, the pebbly beach here is an understandably popular place for a dip. There's even a shower at the café for bathers.

☛ TROODOS MOUNTAINS

The Troodos chain in west central Cyprus is the island's principal upland (note that it is pronounced more "tro-dos," than "true-doss"). The mountains provide many things to many people: a breath of fresh air for hot and flustered visitors and locals, a splendid collection of tiny Byzantine churches, wonderful walking trails, and most important of all, much of the island's fresh water.

It was the British who pioneered the idea of using the Troodos as a resort area. In the days when the empire boasted many tropical outposts, the British developed what they termed hill-stations — bolt holes for rest and recreation where servicemen could get away from the hot, arid plains to cool off amid the mountain greenery. They simply applied the same idea to Cyprus.

The roads climb through foothills with rushing streams and orchards, past villages perched on the slopes, surround-

The roofs and balconies of Kakopetria's restored houses bring out the subtle hues of local stone.

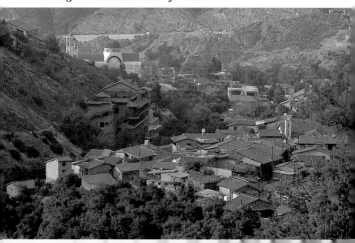

ed at higher altitudes by pine forest. Monks and EOKA fighters have also found refuge here, and the monasteries are now joined by resort hotels and spas, with even a little winter skiing near the town of Troodos.

Platres to Troodos

At an altitude of 1,128 m (3,700 ft), **Pano Platres** makes a good base for visiting the whole Troodos region. The little town occupies a charming and shady mountain site and features several hotels, restaurants, and shops.

The most popular pastime here is walking, and the Cyprus Tourism Organization has marked several walking trails in the mountains that appeal to most ability levels. Stop in at the Platres office for details. The most popular excursion is the 2-km (1-mile) walk to the pretty **Kaledonian Falls,** which may not be in the Niagara league, but is a good reward for an hour's hike. The walk starts at the **Psilon Dhendro** restaurant and trout farm just outside Pano Platres (see page 142) and is well marked.

Some 4 km (2 1/2 miles) from Platres is **Phini**, famous for its traditional Cypriot red-clay ceramics. You can see this ancient craft still being practiced at the homes of a couple of local ladies who will be happy to let you watch them work. There is also a fine folklore museum here.

The larger village of **Omodhos**, recently renovated as one of the Troodos's showpiece villages, lies 6 km (4 miles) south of Phini. It's an attractive place, but its broad main street has become overcommercialized, and the tour buses that now visit destroy the atmosphere they have come to savor. You can find peace and quiet in its Monastery of Timiou Stavrou (The True Cross), however.

It seems that all roads lead to the eponymous resort town of **Troodos,** which at 1,676 m (5,500 ft) is the island's highest resort. In the winter it can provide some decent skiing slopes, while in spring and autumn, it is a good starting point for dedicated ramblers. Avoid midsummer when its main street turns into an overcrowded promenade of kitsch stalls and rumbling tour buses.

Armchair mountaineers may prefer to drive above the town to Cyprus's tallest peak, **Mount Olympus**, at 1,951 m (6,401 ft). For security reasons, you'll have to walk the last few hundred meters up to the giant "golf ball" radar installation on the summit; and the views, even if visibility allows, are not that great. It's a much better idea to gird your loins and tackle one of the two nature trails — the Atalante or the Artemis —

Frescoed Churches

The Troodos Mountains' remarkable painted churches were built mostly between the 11th and the early 16th centuries. For many visitors, the astonishing degree of preservation and the simple but striking beauty of the artwork makes for compulsive viewing. For scholars, the churches provide a fascinating lesson on the history of sacred art, a fact that has been officially recognized by UNESCO (nine churches in the range are on their World Cultural Heritage list). But it's also worth remembering that the primary function of the art was simply to act as religious "cartoon strips" (in the modern sense), teaching the simple, illiterate, and often isolated parishioners the lessons of the Gospels.

The finest concentration of painted churches is in the northeastern part of the Troodos, where Assinou (see page 41), Ayios Nikolaos tis Steyis (see page 71), Galata's two churches (see page 70), and the outstanding Panayia tou Araka are all within a short drive of each other. If the church is closed, you will have to trace the key holder, who is usually the local parish priest. Details are sometimes posted on the church door; otherwise try the nearest café.

that make a circle of the summit and are trail-marked near Troodos, on the way to Mount Olympus.

Kakopetria

In recent years, the Cyprus government has been investing in the reconstruction of traditional village houses as part of its plan to staunch the population flow from the hill villages to the resorts and towns. And nowhere is this effort more to be admired than in Old Kakopetria. This historic part of town, conveniently for visitors, is more or

A mosaic in Kykko, Cyprus's richest and most important monastery for pilgrims.

less one long narrow street that runs parallel to the leafy river. The houses with balconies are being beautifully restored to bring out the subtle russet, amber, and silver hues of the local stone, and with their log-cabin stores, have a real Alpine feel. The town's tour de force is its beautifully restored **wooden mill**. Take the steps down to it, cross the picturesque stone bridge, and enjoy a coffee in a lovely leafy courtyard. The upper floor of the old flour mill is now home to the Maryland at the Mill restaurant (see page 141), while the rest of the building is being developed into a hotel.

Just outside the village is one of the Troodos mountains' most famous frescoed churches (see opposite), **Ayios Nikolaos tis Steyis**, which translates as St. Nicholas of the Roof, and refers to the upper roof of shingles which was built in the 13th century to shelter the older domed roof of tiles. Inside,

The harbor of Paphos, a city on the rise since the tourist boom following the 1974 partition.

its oldest frescoes date from the church's foundation in the 11th century.

Galata

Galata boasts two UNESCO-listed churches (see the box on page 70), both dating from the 16th century. Heading south from Kakopetria, drive slowly and you will spot one of them, the Panayia tis Podythou, from the main road. There is a turn-off at this point. It is not as well preserved, nor is the artwork as detailed as at some Troodos churches, but it still features some outstanding images. In summer, the churches are open most of the day and the key holder is usually trotting between here and the church of **Archangelos**, about 200 meters away. Archangelos is smaller and of less interest than Podythou but is still worth a visit. Continue into Galata itself to visit a small folk art museum and a restored Ottoman *khan*.

West to Kykko

The road west from Troodos winds through pine groves, vineyards, and orchards of apples, pears, peaches, cherries, almonds, and walnuts to **Prodhromos**, 1,402 m (4,600 ft) above sea level. Its modest hotels and restaurants are popular with hikers and jeep safaris.

Farther downhill is **Pedhoulas**, which is famous for its cherries and a popular destination in spring for Cypriots who flock to see the thousands of trees in blossom. Below the main church, the smaller, 15th-century **Archangel Michael** church occupies an impressive site on a steep hill overlooking the valley and features some remarkable frescoes.

Kykko Monastery, some 20 km (12 miles) from Pedhoulas, sits proudly remote from the world on a mountainside surrounded by pine forest. The drive here offers marvelous views of the mountains at every twist and turn. Kykko is the richest and most important monastery for pilgrims on the island. Founded in 1094 by a hermit, it grew in prestige when Emperor Alexis Comnenius gave it a rich land grant and an icon of the Virgin Mary said to have been painted by St. Luke. Having survived several fires, the icon

---

The Wishing Tree

The tradition of tying a handkerchief to a tree at a sacred site is common in the Near and Middle East. The handkerchief is given as a votive offering (akin to lighting a candle in a church in the West to accompany a prayer of thanks or devotion), and goes back to the days when handkerchiefs were valuable items.

---

is now covered in gilded silver. Its legendary rain-making powers still bring in farmers to pray in time of drought. Everyday offerings left here range from expensive jewelry to simple *ex votos* of beeswax.

If you come at a busy time, you may be dismayed to see a long slow-moving queue of people waiting to enter the church. In fact, this line is comprised of Cypriots who wish to pass directly in front of the iconostasis, kissing the images to show their piety. Other visitors can simply go straight into the church via the rear door. The general reaction on experiencing the intense glitter and exuberant ornamentation of the church is one of astonishment. In fact, aside from the precious icon and a few other pieces, there is little of historical or significant artistic value here, but for the lay visitor this hardly matters.

Kykko Monastery has been leveled by fire on four occasions; the first occurred in 1365, the last in 1813. Consequently, its buildings are no older than the early 19th century. Recently, they have been covered in scores of glittering new mosaics, though the real jewel in the crown is the excellent museum. Here in cool and calm, you can learn about the history of the foundation and see some of its finest treasures.

Kykko is also famous for including Archbishop Makarios among its novices (the great man is buried on the hill above the monastery known as Throni). In the 1950s, Kykko was reputed to have served as a communications and supply base for the EOKA movement, and so became a symbol of the official Cypriot nationalist struggle. On the road to the monastery, you will see brown-and-white tourist attraction signs pointing to old EOKA hideouts.

PAPHOS

Paphos has been transformed by the tourist boom that followed the 1974 partition. Facilities expanded at a lightning rate, turning a sleepy fishing port into a full-fledged Mediterranean seaside resort. But visitors who want to do more than just lie in the sun have plenty to occupy them. Paphos was the original island capital and has a wealth of historic sites. It is also a comfortable base from which to explore the western mountain villages and monasteries and the beautiful nature trails of the Akamas Peninsula.

Legend attributes the founding of Palea (Old) Paphos, the original city, to the priest-king Cinyras. In Mycenaean times, a temple to Aphrodite was built here, 16 km (10 miles) from today's Paphos, and the city-kingdom gained renown as the center of Aphrodite's cult. The last king of Palea Paphos, Nicocles, established the new port town of Nea (New) Paphos late in the fourth century B.C., though Palea Paphos remained the

The extensive ruins of Saranda Kolones, a castle built by French crusaders at the end of the 12th century.

center of Aphrodite worship until the fourth century A.D. Within 100 years of its founding, Nea Paphos surpassed Salamis as the chief city of Cyprus. However, earthquakes in 332 and 342 and Saracen attacks in the seventh century forced most of the population inland to Ktima. Following the Genoese invasion in 1372, Nea Paphos was completely abandoned.

For centuries, Paphos languished as a miserable unsanitary seaport. However, the population gradually increased to over 2,000 by the late 19th century. It continued to grow and prosper, and in spite of some damage during the 1974 war, it bounced back to attract not only tourists but also new Cypriot settlers.

Kato (Lower) Paphos

Kato Paphos, along the seaside, is where most visitors stay, and thus is heavily developed. However, the harbor still pro-

vides a picturesque haven for fishing boats and sailing vessels as it curves around a jetty to the old **Paphos Fort**. Over the centuries, virtually the same masonry has been set up, knocked down, and rearranged to form a Roman fort, a feudal castle, a Turkish tower, and a British warehouse for salt. It's now an empty shell but worth the small entrance fee for its rooftop views.

The Tombs of the Kings — a city for the dead now explored by the living.

Just across the harbor parking lot (no formal entrance or signs) lies several of Paphos's ancient historic monuments. The first, marked by its trademark arch, is the **Byzantine c Castle**, popularly known as *Saranda Kolones* (40 columns) after the number of granite columns found lying around here. Excavations have since established its true identity as a castle built by French crusaders at the end of the 12th century and destroyed by earthquake in 1222. Its large square keep had a tower at each corner, surrounded by a dry moat and thick exterior walls with eight bastions.

With the harbor on your left, walk toward the large modern shed-like building in the distance. Sheltered beneath, you will find the famous **Paphos mosaics**. These splendid decorative floors were uncovered in the remains of wealthy Roman villas (third century A.D.) of Nea Paphos and constitute the most important group of mosaics in Cyprus. The "houses" are named after the mosaics' most prominent motif.

The **House of Dionysos** displays the god of wine returning from India on a chariot drawn by two panthers. This and other scenes, such as Dionysos counseling moderation to the nymph Akme drinking wine from a bowl, and King Icarios of Athens getting shepherds drunk with their first taste of wine, were customary decorations for the dining room.

The **House of Aion** has a spectacular five-paneled mosaic. The large central panel depicts Aion, god of eternity, judging a beauty contest between a somewhat smug-looking Queen Cassiopeia (the winner) and the unhappy, prettier Nereides water nymphs.

There are two more areas sometimes open to the public, the Villa of Theseus and the House of Orpheus, but for the present both are closed for long-term restoration.

A short walk north leads to the **Odeon** (marked clearly by a lighthouse), a reconstructed amphitheater of the second century A.D. In a picturesque hillside setting, it seats 1,250 spectators for regular open-air shows.

Kato Paphos to Ktima

From the road entrance to the harbor, Apostolos Pavlos (St. Paul's) Avenue climbs to the excavated site of a fourth-century A.D. early Christian basilica. Among the ruins of a huge seven-aisled church, you can make out mosaic pavements with floral and geometric patterns, Corinthian capitals, and columns of green-and-white marble imported from Greece. Arabic graffiti on some of the columns dates from the invasion, which destroyed the basilica in 653. One of the columns is still described as **St. Paul's Pillar**, to which the apostle was traditionally (but apocryphally) tied and lashed 39 times for preaching the Gospel.

Amid the ruins is the handsome post-Byzantine **Ayia Kyriaki church** (also known as Khrysopolitissa), at which Catholic and Anglican services are held. Note just to the north of the Christian sanctuaries the tiny twin-domed ruined Turkish baths, with an ancient gnarled tree trunk pushing up through the masonry.

A little farther up the hill is the strange sight (to western eyes) of a tree festooned with hundreds of handkerchiefs and rags. It marks the **Catacomb of Ayia Solomoni**, once regarded as a spot where disease could be cured by miracles, and still doing a good trade with believers if today's votive offerings in the tiny rock-cut chapel below are indicative.

Northwest of what was Nea Paphos (off the road to the beach resort of Coral Bay) is the ancient community's necropolis, known as the **Tombs of the Kings.** The title is a misnomer, as these subterranean burial chambers were built from the third century B.C. to the third century A.D. — a period when Paphos had no kings. But many of the tombs are imposing enough to suggest that they were at least the resting places of the Ptolemy dynasty's most important local officials. This "city of the dead," an imitation of the city of the living, gives a rare insight into the residential architecture of Nea Paphos: spacious courtyards with Doric columns and decorative entablatures. It is an atmospheric place and great fun to explore (tombs 3, 4, and 8 are the best), though do be careful as there are sudden unprotected drops.

Kitma's Eliades Collection is an atmospheric slice of old Cypriot life.

Ktima

Set on a hilltop above the resort, Ktima, as this upper part of Paphos is known, is a breath of fresh air and everyday reality. There is a colorful daily fruit-and-vegetable market and a plethora of souvenir stalls in the old covered market. After shopping, you can relax with a meal or a drink, enjoying the excellent views down to the coast.

It is a 10- to 15-minute walk to the two small museums in the town center. The most popular is the Ethnographical Museum, known as the **Eliades Collection** on Exo Vrysis Street near the Bishop's Palace. Set in a charming 19th-century house, it combines prehistoric fossils, classical antiquities, and Cypriot folklore of the 18th and 19th centuries. In the garden, carved into the bedrock, burial chambers from the third century B.C. have been uncovered.

Just across the road from here, in a wing of the Bishop's Palace, is the **Byzantine Museum,** which comprises a gallery of icons salvaged from local chapels.

You'll need transport to reach the **Paphos District Archaeological Museum,** which is out on the road to Limassol (Gina Dighenis Avenue). It houses some fine sculptures found in the Roman Villa of Theseus (see above). Carved in white marble imported from the Aegean, they include fine statues of Demeter and also Asclepios (the Greek master of medicine) feeding an egg to the snake coiled around his staff. Adjacent, notice the bizarre pottery hot-water bottles from the first century A.D., specially molded to fit all parts of the body, and used for curative purposes.

East of Paphos

Just east of town on the road to Paphos Airport is the village of Yeroskipos (pronounced "Yer-ross-key-poo"), which means "Sacred Garden" and is dedicated to Aphrodite. Once pilgrims from Nea Paphos stopped off here on their way to the goddess's temple at Palea Paphos; today, they stop to buy souvenirs or Cypriot Delight, which is manufactured at several roadside outlets.

The 11th-century church of **Ayia Paraskevi** is a rare island example of a five-domed basilica. Inside are some 15th-century murals and a much-revered icon from the same period, with a *Virgin and Child* on one side and a *Crucifixion* on the reverse.

In a restored house nearby is the likeable and informative **Museum of Folk Art**. Typical of a rich Cypriot's villa in the 18th century, it has an upper story surrounded by handsome wooden balconies. Museum displays include elaborate gourds made into unlikely items (such as devices to help keep children afloat when swimming), domestic and farming implements, rural costumes, furniture, and many interesting bygones.

The five-domed basilica of Ayia Paraskevi is a rare ancient survivor, stranded in the middle of modern-day Yeroskipos.

From Yeroskipos, continue east for about 12 km (8 miles) and turn off at Kouklia, once Palea Paphos, where the cult of Aphrodite took place. As described by Homer, the love-goddess rites flourished here at the **Sanctuary of Aphrodite** from very early times. Alas, little romance can be found in the ruins, and Aphrodite seems to have wafted away on a zephyr, the way she came. Most of the valuable finds from the sanctuary have been taken to Nicosia, though a copy of the famous mosaic of *Leda and the Swan* remains in situ. The distinctive and sturdy Château de Covocle (originally a Lusignan fort, and then a Turkish manor house and farm) is now home to the collection of the **Palea Paphos Museum**. Its prize exhibit is the large conical stone that symbolizes the goddess (her beauty was too great to represent literally) and was the epicenter of Aphrodite worship.

North of Paphos

The beaches in Paphos are less than remarkable, so it's no surprise that many visitors are prepared to travel 10 km (6 miles) north to the nicer sands, plentiful water sports, and beachside dining of the Coral Bay resort.

An alternative route north is to head inland toward Polis. Just 10 km (6 miles) north of Paphos, the **Monastery of Ayios Neophytos** dominates a peaceful, wooded slope. Its church has some fine 15th- and 16th-century frescoes and icons, but the main focus, on the hillside opposite the church, is the 12th-century **Englistra** (Hermitage), around which the monastery grew up. The saintly historian and theologian Neophytos (1134–1214) hacked this cave-dwelling out of the rock with his own hands and then supervised the wonderful frescoes which decorate the chapel, sanctuary, and cell. One scene shows Neophytos himself, flanked by the archangels Michael and Gabriel.

On the north coast, the town of **Polis** stands where the ancient city-kingdom of Marion once boasted rich gold and copper mines. The small village center has been attractively restored with a pleasant if rather touristy row of cafés and restaurants. Polis is a gateway to the fishing port and burgeoning, though still relatively low-key, beach resort of **Latchi**. A dozen or so restaurants, cafés, and bars cluster around the picturesque harbor and, to either side, are hard sand, shingle, and pebble beaches. Water sports are on offer, while the harbor is the watery gateway to the Akamas Peninsula (see page 83).

Romantics should head farther west until the road ends at a parking lot by the **Loutra tis Aphroditis** (Baths of

Aphrodite). It's an easy 5-minute walk to a small, shaded natural pool and springs set in a cool green glade where our local heroine bathed to rejuvenate herself. Mere mortals are not allowed to cool off here, but at the other side of the parking lot, a steep path leads down to a couple of narrow pebble beaches with crystal-clear shallow water. Alternatively, if you would like to walk in the Akamas, marked paths lead off from Aphrodite's Baths.

The **Akamas Peninsula** is one of the few unspoiled wildernesses left on the island and is currently a major battleground between environmentalists and developers. See page 114 for details of guided tours in this region.

The crowds of Paphos have not yet discovered the simple seaside pleasures of Latchi.

WHAT TO DO

C yprus is an active, lively place where there is plenty to do beyond sightseeing. Sporting activities benefit from a great climate and amazingly clear coastal waters. Entertainment ranges from some of the Mediterranean's hottest nightclubs (Ayia Napa likes to style itself as the new Ibiza) to more sedate folklore at the village festivals, and even a play or concert in the grand setting of an ancient open-air theater.

SPORTS

Cyprus's beaches may not have the best sands, but they do boast crystal-clear unpolluted seas. Ramblers can find solitude and marvelous scenery in the unspoiled mountain country of the interior or along the rugged Akamas Peninsula.

Extreme Sports

For many people over 35, taking a vacation in Ayia Napa would be an extreme sport. Now you can augment the hazards of non-stop partying with bungee jumping above Nissi Beach. The drop is 45 m (150 ft) with an optional water touch.

Just as terrifying is the Slingshot, claimed to be the highest and fastest ride in the world. Somewhat akin to being strapped to a missile, riders are propelled to a height of 100 m (300 ft) in a breathtaking 1.3 seconds. There are no prizes for guessing that this is also located in Ayia Napa!

Golf

Golf is not a game associated with Cyprus, but two excellent new courses have recently been created and are worth seeking out. Secret Valley, near Aphrodite's Birthplace, is, as its name suggests, tucked away in a lovely hidden location. Tsada, northeast of Paphos, is also very attractive. Both are

6,000-meter (18,000-ft), 18-hole courses with all the usual fa-cilities. You must produce a handicap certificate to play (men 28, ladies 36). Greens fees, by northern European standards, are very reasonable; call (06) 642774 for both courses.

Watersports

Scuba divers and snorkelers are the major beneficiaries of Cyprus's limpid seas, which are perfect for underwater pho-tography. In water temperatures ranging from 16°C (60°F) to 27°C (80°F), you can explore submerged cliffs, valleys, and caves, and get close-up views of sea anemones and sponges, exotic colored fish, and crustaceans.

You will find qualified diving centers with rental equipment and instruction at Paphos, Coral Bay, Latchi, Larnaca, Limassol, Ayia Napa, and Protaras.

Windsurfing and water-skiing are available everywhere, with equipment for rent at public and hotel beaches. Experienced windsurfers should head for the capes for strong breezes. Other activities such as jetskiing and parasailing are available at all

Fun in the sun and sea — there are watersports galore in Cyprus. Here, a group gets their thrills on a "water banana."

resorts. Serious sailors can hire craft from the marinas at Paphos, Larnaca, or Limassol.

Walking and Hiking

The Troodos Mountains and the Akamas Peninsula are ideal for walking, though most people will find hiking in these areas too strenuous, or just plain uncomfortable, in summer.

View to a thrill: hang gliding over the spectacular Cape Greco viewpoint.

If you want to go it alone, the Cyprus Tourism Organization distributes many maps and information on local itineraries. Try the Paphos office for the Akamas Peninsula, and the Platres office for the Troodos Mountains, or ask at any office for a copy of the excellent Nature Trails brochure which details and maps a number of popular walks all over the island. In the Baths of Aphrodite parking lot, there's a seasonal tourist office which has details of walking trails; it is also from here that marked paths lead off into the Akamas. On the Aphrodite and Adonis trails, plants have been marked along the way with numbers and are identified in the free booklet *Nature Trails of the Akamas*. Sunflower Guides produces a book on walking in Cyprus that is on sale on the island and in the UK.

For organized walking tours of the Akamas, try the well-respected Exalt Travel (Tel. 06-243803). Their adventurous trekking program takes in dry river beds, lunar-like landscapes of high chalk plateaus, refreshing waterfalls, and the spectacular giant limestone Avagas Gorge. You don't need to have any experience, just as long as you are reasonably healthy and have a decent pair of training shoes.

Experienced hikers in search of adventure deep in the Troodos may enjoy the nature trails that set out from the well-organized forestry station of Stavros tis Psokas, north of Kykko. There's a hostel up here that you will need to reserve in advance; Tel. (06) 332144. Less intimidating are the Atalante and Artemis trails (12 km/8 miles and 7 km/4 miles, respectively), which enable you to walk around Mount Olympus (see page 70). An easy but rewarding short trek leads to the Kaledonia Falls (see page 69).

Winter Sports

Lifts provide access to several ski runs on Mount Olympus, and more are being developed. Cross-country skiing is also possible. Depending on snow conditions (which are usually poor), the ski season runs from January to late March. It is not worth making a special trip to Cyprus for the snow, but skiing in the morning and swimming in the afternoon is a great novelty.

ACTIVITIES FOR CHILDREN

Most of Cyprus's resorts are marketed as family destinations, and with long clean beaches and almost guaranteed sunshine, it is a good place to bring the kids. The Cypriots, like most Southern Mediterraneans, love children, and safety considerations aside, there are few, if any, restrictions on where they can go.

If you are bored with the beach, but not with the water, there are three water parks to explore. **WaterWorld**, just outside Ayia Napa at Ayia Thekla, claims to be the biggest theme water park in Europe. It has over 20 rides ranging from high-speed thrill chutes to the Lazy River. Most impressive of all is the Drop to Atlantis, where you crash through various sound-and-light effects before the final splash. Greek columns, statues, and fountains provide the theme. There are two other water parks: Wet 'n' Wild, just east of Limmasol, is larger and wilder than Watermania on the western side of Limmasol at Fassouri.

Luna Park is a term used in Cyprus whenever a few fairground-style attractions are assembled in one place. These are modest places, but the biggest and best is La Luna Fun Fair in Ayia Napa. It's a bona fide amusement park with lots of rides for all the family.

Other activities that might appeal to kids are glass-bottomed boat rides from Paphos or Latchi, and the Paphos Aquarium with over 50 small tanks of colorful sea creatures.

It's generally not a good idea to drag children around archaelogical sites, but a possible exception to this rule is the Tombs of the Kings in Paphos (see page 78). Here your little ones can pretend that they are Indiana Jones, delving into dark spooky holes and racing through some spectacular Classical courtyards with Doric pillars. Beware of sudden deep unfenced holes.

Make a splash! Water parks are among the best attractions for children off the beach in Cyprus.

SHOPPING

The quality of most tourist-oriented shops in Cyprus is low, tending toward the cheapest forms of imported tat rather than building on the craft strengths of the island. If possible, your first stop should always be at the nearest Cyprus Handicraft Center, which acts as a showcase for

> **Never use the term Turkish delight — simply call it by its Greek name** *loukoumi* **("loo-koo-me").**

the best of the island's artisans. Compared with what is on sale elsewhere, goods in here are expensive because they are hand-made. You will find them at the following locations: Paphos: 64 Apostolos Pavlos Avenue (main road from Kato Paphos to Ktima); Limassol: 25 Themidhos Street; Larnaca: Kosma Lysioti, just off the Foinikades Promenade; Nicosia (South): Laiki Yitonia.

Traditional shop hours are from 8am to 1pm and from 4 to 7pm (2:30 to 5:30pm in winter). In the tourist centers, shops stay open for longer hours.

Best Buys

Basketry. The choices range from small baskets in decorative shapes and colors to large articles in rush or cane.

Brass. Look for candlesticks, ashtrays, small boxes, religious ornaments, and trays.

Ceramics. By the standard of the beautiful pieces available in the Greek islands, most Cypriot ceramics are crude and garish. Seek out artisans who look back to antiquity for inspiration, creating charming animal figurines, little vessels, and terracotta statuettes. If you can't find them, ask at the local tourist office. The functional wares of Kornos and Phini in-

clude attractive hand-thrown wine and oil jars.

Copperware. Dating from over 3,000 years ago, the copper industry remains a source of Cypriot pride. There are all manner of hand-crafted wares, including copper pots, saucepans, and bowls.

Embroidery. Shops all over Cyprus sell the island's most important cottage industry items — fine linen table-cloths, doilies, runners, and handkerchiefs stitched with intricate geometric patterns of Lefkara (see page 53).

Put on a happy face: masks are among the many treasures for sale in Yeroskipos.

Food and Wine. "Cypriot Delight" or *loukoumi* is a specialty of Yeroskipos — though shops all over the island sell it. You may want to carry home Cypriot olives or sealed packets of the local cheese, *halloumi*. Of the many wines and liqueurs produced on Cyprus, the most popular gift is Commandaria, the sweet red dessert wine.

Icons. Not the real thing, of course, but a whole gamut of copies are available, from the exquisite works of nuns and monks such as Father Kallinikos (see page 55) to cheaper items on sale in most gift shops.

Jewelry. You can find good quality silver and gold, the latter almost always 18-karat (as opposed to Greece's more customary 14-karat). You will also find a load of rubbish in the resorts, so beware. Reputable jewelers will always provide a certificate of authenticity.

Leather Goods. Manufactured locally, shoes and sandals are reasonably priced on Cyprus, though they often lack styling.

ENTERTAINMENT

Most resorts have a publication that lists events of interest during your stay. Another good resource is the "What's On" section of the *Cyprus Mail* or *Sunday Mail*.

Nightlife

Nightlife in Cyprus is usually fairly unsophisticated, comprising an evening at a restaurant or taverna, then moving on to a bar. Most of the resorts have karaoke bars, loud live-music bars, and a nightclub or two. Ayia Napa is the island's party town, with scores of live-music bars and some 15 nightclubs that cater to a wild Anglo-Scandinavian 18–30 crowd.

Folklore Shows

Most hotels offer weekly folklore shows with Cypriot-costumed performers singing and dancing to traditional and classic Greek tunes (by the end of your vacation, you will be sick of hearing *Zorba's Dance*). Visitors are invariably encouraged to get up and dance along — whether they want to or not — and nobody objects to missteps. Many tavernas also have Greek dancing on a regular or semi-regular basis. One local specialty that is worth looking out for is the glass-balancing routine. A dancer will have an empty glass placed upside down on his head by one of his colleagues and dance a few steps to show his balancing agility. It may not be terribly impressive with just one on his head, but by the time his colleagues have balanced a 30-glass tower (each interleaved with a beer mat), and the dancer is still coming back for more, the crowd is open-mouthed. The best place to see this on a regular basis is Demokritos in Paphos (see page 74). A less common, but even more incredible, glass routine involves placing a glass, this time half full of drink, into an old-fashioned wooden sieve. The sieve is at first gently swung from side to side, then in an instant it is furiously rotated through all sorts of circles while the dancer takes on the appearance of a whirling dervish. Incredibly, centrifugal force keeps the glass and liquid perfectly in place, and the audience dry too.

Historical Entertainment Venues

The most memorable and distinctive evening's entertainment on offer is a night at the amphitheater. The Paphos Odeon stages plays (in English), while the magnificently situated amphitheater at Kourion is a wonderful place to catch a Shakespearean play or classical drama, or to hear some jazz. If you are staying at Limassol, or even Paphos, it's well worth the effort. Rent a cushion, if possible, or take along

something soft to sit on. Out of high season, you may well need a sweater, too.

Another pleasant historical outdoor entertainment venue is the castle at Larnaca with performances of dance and theater as part of the Larnaca Festival in July.

Traditional dancing makes for a festive evening in Ayia Napa.

Festivals and Holy Days

January *Ta Fota.* On Epiphany Day (6 January), bishops bless the waters in all the seaside towns, throwing their Holy Crosses into the sea. Boys dive for them.

February/March *Carnival.* Limassol's ten-day long celebration features fancy-dress balls and a spate of parades. It's not Rio, but it's fun.

March/April *Good Friday.* Solemn Orthodox masses take place all over Cyprus, with a procession of the Holy Sepulchre in main streets and squares.

Easter. A midnight service takes place on the Saturday before Easter, when people light their candles from the priest's, moving around the church and chanting the litany. Once the service is over, spectacular firework displays begin. On Easter Sunday, high masses celebrate the resurrection of Christ.

May/June *Kataklismos.* The Festival of the Flood coincides with Pentecost, and this two-day holiday harks back to ancient times, when Cypriots convened at temples to worship and sacrifice to Adonis and Aphrodite. Today, there are excursions to the beach, parties, games, colorful parades, and competitions — especially at Paphos.

July *Larnaca Festival.* During this historically oriented festival, dance and theater performances are staged at the castle in Larnaca.

August *Assumption of the Virgin.* On 15 August, the faithful gather at the leading monasteries and churches. This is the most important day in the Greek religious festival calendar. Beware: crowds are massive.

September *Nicosia Arts Festival.* This two-week long event features everything from art exhibitions and folk dancing to avant-garde ballet and rock concerts.

Limassol Wine Festival. A fortnight of wine-tastings, dancing, and folklore shows. (Note: This event may begin in late August.)

Ayia Napa Festival. This festival of folklore, music, dance, and theater has been going strong for over 15 years and attracts large crowds.

EATING OUT

The food of Cyprus will be familiar to anyone who has visited Greece. Basically, it is comprised of grilled meats and fish, salads, and a small selection of specialty casserole dishes. Strangely, vegetables, though grown in abundance in the east of the island, rarely find their way to resort restaurant tables.

At its best, Cypriot cooking is a simple, hearty, and healthy cuisine. Unfortunately, with mass tourism has come that dreaded, bland hybrid called "international cuisine," and worse still, mass catering has impacted badly on the local food. Bright industrial-pink factory-produced *taramasalata* and imitation crab sticks are now passed off as part of a traditional fish *meze* (see below), and a request for boiled potatoes, instead of the ubiquitous french fries, is greeted with incredulity. Many tourist-oriented restaurants now simply cook to a price, and if you are at all serious about your food, you should choose very carefully where you eat. Ask the locals, go where they eat, and see our recommendations on page 138.

Etiquette

As opposed to Greece, where you're encouraged to go into the kitchen to point out what you'd like to eat, Cypriot eating houses usually expect you to order from the menu (which is always translated into English). Some traditional Cypriot tavernas have no menu, just a set meal, and you pay a fixed price for whatever is being served that night. Trust them and enjoy your meal. Another difference from eating out in the Greek islands (a welcome one to most northern Europeans) is that the food is generally served hot, instead of lukewarm. Cypriots are known for their generosity and restaurateurs are no exception. In a good local restaurant, fresh fruit, Greek coffee, perhaps even the local wine, may well be on the house. You should return the gesture with an appropriate tip.

Note that the terms taverna and restaurant are often used loosely in Cyprus, though the former implies an informal, even rustic traditional eating and drinking establishment.

Meze

Meze, strictly speaking, are appetizers, though the meze which many restaurants in Cyprus offer indicates a full meal (in fact a meal and a half!). A typical Cypriot meze comprises some 20-plus small dishes with a mixture of appetizers and small portions of main courses. It is an excellent crash course in Cypriot food and is usually good value, though invariably it must be ordered by a minimum of two people. The choice is usually meat meze or fish meze. Don't be afraid to ask what it comprises. Keep in mind that although the portions are small, they do add up. Unless you are a big eater, you may feel uncomfortable the next day.

FAST FOOD

Cypriot fast food generally means a pita bread stuffed with *sheftalia* (like a mini-burger) or *souvlaki*, a kebab of grilled cubes of fresh lamb or goat, plus salad, and a yogurt dressing. The ingredients will be fresh and the sheftalia will be homemade with local herbs. Your dish will be prepared especially for you, and it will be completely delicious. You will get these snacks at small "hole-in-the-wall" places or in local-style cafés. It is the cheapest and arguably one of the healthiest ways of filling up.

Starters

Common to nearly all restaurants serving Cypriot-style food are four dips: taramas/taramasalata, a pink fish-roe paste which should be made with olive oil and lemon juice and thickened with mashed potato, or softened bread; *talatoura*, a Cypriot variant of the Greek *tzatziki* (yogurt with cucumber, crushed garlic, and fresh mint); *tahini*, a sesame-seed paste with garlic; and *hummos*, a purée of chick-peas, olive oil, and spices. To accompany these dips, you'll be served either fresh Cypriot sesame-seed bread (koulouri), or pita bread. Take care not to fill up immediately! Another well-known Greek starter is koupepia, better known as *dolmades* or *dolmadaki* — vine leaves stuffed with rice and lamb, flavored with mint. That other Greek staple, stuffed vegetables, is not common in Cyprus.

Two more permanent items on the starter section of a menu are *lounza*, a thinly sliced fillet of smoked pork and *halloumi*, a Cypriot ewe's-milk cheese. Both of these may be served hot (charcoal-grilled or fried) or cold, and are often offered as a combination. Much less common on restaurant menus is *loukanika*, a delicious Cypriot smoked sausage (of the British link variety, as opposed to the Continental slicing kind).

Local soups are not common on restaurant menus (aside from the ubiquitous vegetable soup, which usually means "yesterday's leftovers"). But if you do get the chance, try *avgolemono*, a lemon-flavored chicken broth thickened with egg and served

Enjoy a fresh crisp Greek Salad and a starter of creamy tzatziki dip.

with rice of Greek origin. It often appears on the menu, but frustratingly, is not usually available.

Another rarity to look out for is *kypriakes ravioles,* Cypriot ravioli stuffed with halloumi, eggs, and mint.

Souvlakia are kebabs — skewered pieces of either lamb, goat, chicken, beef, or pork, grilled over charcoal and eaten as a starter, a main course, or simply as a snack.

Fish and Shellfish

As offshore catches become smaller and smaller, the choice of seafood becomes more limited and prices increase accordingly. Octopus (*chtapodi*) is often served in a red wine sauce. Prawns (*garidhes*), battered squid (*kalamari*), and spiny lobster are common menu items, but may be frozen rather than fresh. This should be indicated on the menu but, if in doubt, ask.

Fresh fish that is generally available is swordfish (*xifias*), red mullet (*barbounia*), red snapper (*sinagrida*), gilt-head bream (*tsipoura*), and sometimes whitebait (*marides*). Fish is usually simply barbecued.

The specialty of the Troodos mountains is farmed trout — either smoked, sautéed (perhaps with slivered almonds), or *au bleu* (poached with clarified butter).

Meat Dishes and Vegetables

Almost without exception, every restaurant that serves Greek-Cypriot food in the tourist resorts has a section on its menu entitled Cypriot Specialties. Invariably, it comprises the following dishes: *moussaka*, a layered dish of minced meat, eggplant, potatoes, with a bechamel-like sauce and spices; *afelia*, a tender pork stew made with red wine, cumin, and coriander seeds; *kleftiko*, oven-roasted lamb with mint, the traditional Sunday lunch for the locals; *stifado*, a catch-all term for a stew of tomatoes, herbs, olive oil, and vinegar which usually features beef; keftedhes, meat balls flavored with herbs, usually coriander and cumin. Less common but well worth trying is tavas, lamb or pork cooked in a clay pot with vegetables and spices. A variety of plain grilled steaks and chops also feature on all menus.

Vegetable dishes and accompaniments are scarce. In the tourist quarters, everything is served with french fries and either Greek salad or "Village-style salad," which are one and the same and feature lettuce or shredded cabbage, cucumbers, tomatoes, perhaps olives, and always a thick slice or two of feta cheese.

In more authentic restaurants, you should be able to get black-eyed beans (*louvia*) or *fasolia,* which may also be black-eyed beans or large white beans, usually served cold in a delicious tomato and onion sauce; green beans or peas; tomatoes; courgettes (zucchini); and eggplant. Look out too for *kolokassia,* which comes from the taro root, a relative of the yam.

Desserts and Sweets

Dessert usually means ice cream or fruit. Go for the latter. Depending on the season, you'll be able to try the island's outstanding honeydew and cantaloupe melons, watermelon, cherries, peaches, figs, apricots, oranges, tangerines, plums, grapes, pomegranates, and more.

Cypriot sweets are rarely offered as dessert after a meal, but are sold separately in cafés or at specially set up stalls. Beware, for they are very sweet indeed. Honey and nuts flavor both *baklava,* a strudel-like pastry, and *kataïfi,* a pastry which resembles shredded wheat. Another mouth-watering specialty is *loukoumades,* a kind of sweet, puffy deep-fried doughnut dipped in syrup.

Coffee

Unless you specify Greek coffee, you will probably be served Nescafé; not necessarily the brand, but the generic Greek term for instant coffee. In a do-it-yourself fashion, you are provided hot water with a sachet of instant powder. However, more and more places are offering filter coffee or the ubiquitous cappuccino.

If you would prefer the local stuff, order *kafé elleniko* (Greek coffee), or simply *kahve* in the north. You will have to specify sweet (*gliko*), medium-sweet (*metrio*), or without sugar (*sketo*). Greek coffee is always taken black, and accompanied by a glass of water. Don't disturb or drink the thick grounds at the bottom of the cup.

Oristeh! How can I help you/What would you like?

Wines

Cyprus wines have been renowned since antiquity. Foremost among them is the sweet red Commandaria, originally produced for the Knights of St. John at Kolossi (see page 63). Celebrated as an apéritif or dessert wine, it is similar to Madeira and worth trying even if you normally don't like sweet wines. Sweet and dry wines of the sherry type are another Cypriot specialty.

Cypriot table wines are constantly improving in quality, though you would never guess so from the house wines that are routinely put in front of visitors. By northern European standards, the quality is very low and some are virtually undrinkable. It is always worth paying a little more and ordering a branded bottle. In a decent restaurant the waiter will help you with a recommendation. Bella Pais, a rather bubbly white, makes a good apéritif or dessert wine. Duc de Nicosie is the closest a Cyprus wine comes to champagne, and is produced using the traditional French method.

Other Alcoholic Drinks

As an after-dinner drink, you may well be offered a *zivania*, Cyprus fire water. Distilled from the grape detritus, it is very similar to the drink called *raki* in Greece. Treat it with caution! The other famous Greek drink enjoyed in Cyprus is *ouzo*, a clear aniseed-flavored spirit which turns milky with the addition of water. (Confusingly, this drink is called *raki* by the Turkish).

The Cypriots are also known for their brandy. If you are going to drink it straight, go for one of the better-known, more expensive brands, to avoid throat burn. A much more common use for local brandy is as the base for a brandy sour, the traditional island sundowner.

The local lager (always referred to as beer), Keo, is very good. Carlsberg is also brewed (to its original Continental strength) on the island.

Cypriot "fast food" is prepared with the freshest of ingredients, and is always delicious.

To Help You Order...

The following words and phrases should be of assistance when ordering food and drink. You may want to purchase a copy of the *Berlitz European Menu Reader* or the *Berlitz Greek Phrase Book and Dictionary*; both have a comprehensive glossary of Greek wining and dining.

Could we have a table?	**Tha boroúsame na échoume éna trapézi?**		
I'd like a/an/some ...	**Tha íthela ...**		
beer	**mía bíra**	meat	**kréas**
mineral water	**metallikó neró**	napkin	**petseta**
(iced) water	**(pagoméno) neró**	potatoes	**patátes**
bread	**psomí**	rice	**rízi**
coffee	**éna kafé**	salad	**mía saláta**
cutlery	**macheropírouna**	soup	**mía soúpa**
dessert	**éna glikó**	sugar	**záchari**
fish	**psári**	tea	**éna tsäï**
fruit	**froúta**	milk	**gála**
glass	**éna potíri**	wine	**krasí**
ice cream	**éna pagotó**		

...and Read the Menu

afelia	pork stew	**lounza**	smoked pork
barbounia	red mullet	**marides**	whitebait
fasolia	beans	**souvlaki**	kebab
garidhes	prawns	**kleftiko**	roast lamb
halloumi	ewe's milk cheese	**keftedhes**	meatballs
stifado	stew (usually beef) with tomatoes	**tsipoura**	gilthead bream
		koupepia	stuffed vine leaves
xifias	swordfish	**tavas**	casserole in clay pot (usually lamb or pork)
kolokassia	taro root ("Cypriot spinach")		

INDEX

HANDY TRAVEL TIPS

An A–Z Summary of Practical Information

A

ACCOMMODATIONS (see CAMPING, YOUTH HOSTELS, and HOTELS AND RESTAURANTS sections)
In the high season (mid-June to October), try to book well in advance. The Cyprus Tourism Organization (see page 126) produces a brochure listing various possibilities in each town. If you arrive without a booking, contact the CTO at the airport or in Nicosia, Larnaca, Limassol, or Paphos for advice.

Hotels Cyprus has hotels in all categories, from five-star luxury havens and comfortable guest houses to pleasant apartment-hotels (classified A, B, C, and Tourist Apartments). Unlike the small Greek islands, accommodation in unregistered private houses is not available. In general, standards are high and prices are reasonable compared with other resorts and islands.

All hotels offer discounts during the low season, which for seaside resorts is from 16 November to 15 March, and for hill resorts from 1 October to 30 June — both excluding the Christmas/New Year and Easter holiday periods.

Villas may be rented through local agencies, or you may inquire at the CTO.

Agrotourism Thanks to a recent initiative by the CTO, some traditional houses in the countryside have been renovated and are now rented out as homes. For further information, ask the CTO for a brochure or contact the Cyprus Agrotourism Company directly: 19 Limassol Avenue, PO Box 4535, 1390 Nicosia, Cyprus. Tel. (02) 337715; fax (02) 339723; web site <www.agrotourism.com.cy>.

I'd like a single/double	**Tha íthela éna monó/dipló domátio**
with bath/shower	**me bánio/dous**
What's the rate per night?	**Piá íne i timí giá mía níkta?**

AIRPORTS

Larnaca International Airport, the principal air gateway to Cyprus, lies 6 km (3 1/2 miles) from Larnaca proper and 50 km (31 miles) from Nicosia. Taxis are available into both cities, while shared taxis and mini-buses, scheduled frequently during the day, provide inexpensive transport for three or more passengers sharing the cost. A few local buses operate daily to Larnaca and Limassol.

A replacement for Nicosia airport — since 1974 designated to be on United Nations territory and no longer used for commercial flights — the Larnaca facility has been modernized and expanded to cope with increased air traffic into the Republic of Cyprus. Larnaca has a duty-free shop, snack bar, restaurant, currency exchange, car-rental agencies, post office, and tourist information office. At peak hours in the high season, check-in counters may be crowded and service somewhat slow, so arrive with plenty of time to spare before flight departure.

Paphos International Airport, 11 km (7 miles) southeast of Paphos proper on the west coast, handles freight and certain scheduled and charter services, easing the congestion at Larnaca. It has a duty-free shop, currency-exchange facilities, and snack-bar restaurants, but at peak times, it is woefully inadequate for the number of tourists it processes.

The airport at Ercan in Northern Cyprus, served by flights from the mainland of Turkey only, has been declared by the Republic of Cyprus a prohibited port of entry and exit.

Porter! Take these bags to the bus/taxi, please. **Parakaló! Pigénete aftés tis aposkevés sto leoforío/taxi.**

ANTIQUITIES

The purchase and export of antiquities is strictly regulated, and export permission must be granted by the Director of the Department of Antiquities, c/o Ministry of Communications and Works, Nicosia. It is illegal to remove antiquities, stones, and other remains from any archaeological site, including the seabed.

B

BICYCLE & MOTORCYCLE RENTAL

You can rent bicycles and motorcycles in all towns. To operate a motorcycle, you must be at least 18 years of age and hold a driver's license (17 year-olds may hire an "auto cycle" of 49cc). It is illegal not to wear a crash helmet (the exception to this rule is for auto cycles under 50cc in built-up areas). However, in practice, very few people wear helmets. Moped hire is very cheap (less than C£5 per day), but check that this does not invalidate your holiday insurance.

Mountain biking, particularly in the Troodos mountains and the Akamas peninsula, is popular and the CTO (see page 126) has a brochure *Cyprus for Cycling*, detailing 19 routes. For more details, call the Cyprus Cycling Federation; Tel. (02) 663341; fax (02) 661150.

BUDGETING FOR YOUR TRIP

Pricewise, Cyprus is above average as a Mediterranean destination; more expensive than most Greek islands and Turkey and some parts of Spain and Southern Portugal, but cheaper than much of mainland Europe. In high season, airfares from Britain cost around £200 and a good four-star hotel's room rate is around C£85 per night. Booking a package, particularly at the last minute, will save you money. Food and drink is cheap (a three-course meal plus drinks usually comes to less than C£10 per person). Car rental starts from C£20 per day (including CDW), while public transport and museum fees are also inexpensive.

C

CAMPING

Official campsites are licensed by the Cyprus Tourism Organization. Most provide electricity, toilets and showers, a food shop, and usually a café. There are seven official sites: Troodos; Polis; Forest Beach, east of Larnaca; Ayia Napa; Governor's Beach, near Limassol; Yeroskipos, near Paphos; and Feggari/Coral Bay, near Paphos. Ask at the nearest CTO office or the local police station for local, unlisted campsites.

Is there a campsite nearby?	**Ipárchi éna méros giá kataskínosi/'camping' edó kondá?**

CAR RENTAL/HIRE (see also DRIVING)

Distances in Cyprus are relatively large and, as many sights are spread out, beyond the reach of public transport, it is definitely worth renting a car.

Budget, Thrifty, Hertz, Avis, and Eurodollar car-rental agencies have offices in the major cities, and representatives at Larnaca and Paphos airports and at the main resorts. Rates are cheap (from around C£15 per day), though you will have to add on another C£5 or so for CDW insurance, and perhaps another C£1 to cover damage to the tires and/or windshield. For a decent family-sized car, you should plan on spending around C£30 per day. In summer, air-conditioning is absolutely essential and well worth the extra money. Cyprus firms generally charge slightly less than international agencies and provide equally good cars and service. Note that the rate always includes unlimited mileage.

Reserve a car ahead of time — especially for the high season. To rent a car, you must have a valid national driver's license (held for at least 3 years) or an International Driving Permit. Depending on the company, the minimum age is 21 to 25. Drivers under 25 will pay an insurance premium. A deposit is usually required, payable by credit card.

I'd like to hire a car (tomorrow)	**Tha íthela na nikiáso éna aftokínito (ávrio)**
for one day/a week.	**giá mía iméra/mía evdomáda.**
Please include full insurance.	**Sas parakaló na simberilávete plíri asfália.**

CLIMATE

Cyprus boasts sunny skies and low humidity almost year-round. On the coast, sea breezes temper the 32°C (90° F) heat of July and August, but in Nicosia you can add on 4 or 5 degrees, and the thermometer has been known to go over 38°C (100°F). Citizens of the capital beat a quick retreat to the coast or Troodos resorts during the hot days of summer.

January and February see snowfalls in the Troodos range — most years enough to allow some skiing. It rains occasionally between October and February, but there's plenty of sun, too, and the sea remains warm enough for swimming.

Average coastal temperatures:

Max	°C	17	17	19	23	26	30	32	33	31	27	22	18
	°F	63	63	66	74	80	86	90	91	88	81	72	66
Min	°C	8	8	9	12	16	19	21	21	20	16	12	9
	°F	46	46	48	55	60	66	70	69	67	61	54	49

CLOTHING

In summer, wear comfortable, loose cotton clothing. July and August nights are very warm, but at other times of the year, they can be cool (so can air-conditioned rooms), so a light sweater is a good idea. In winter months (late November to March), you'll need a raincoat or light winter coat, a warm sweater or jacket, and perhaps a wool outfit or two.

On the beach, toplessness is generally tolerated; nudity in public is unacceptable. Take along a cover-up for the beach-bar — not just for modesty, but because cool breezes blow up. Informality is the general rule, but in the more posh hotels and restaurants, people may dress up in the evening. Men will need long trousers to visit Orthodox monasteries and women must wear a long skirt (often provided) and a modest top.

CRIME & SAFETY

There is still so little crime here that the few robberies which take place make headlines. The island's only violence generally occurs in drunken brawls in Ayia Napa. Cypriots are very honest, but your fellow tourists may not be, so take the usual precautions of locking your rental car and depositing money and jewelry in the hotel safe.

Cyprus

CUSTOMS AND ENTRY REQUIREMENTS (see also MONEY)

Entry Formalities and Custom Controls Nationals of the US, Australia, Canada, Japan, New Zealand, Singapore, and the EU can stay in Cyprus for up to three months without a visa. Legal points of entry are the ports of Larnaca, Limassol, and Paphos, and the international airports of Larnaca and Paphos. Visitors traveling via the airport of Ercan or the ports of Famagusta, Kyrenia, or Karavostasi in Turkish-controlled Northern Cyprus may not cross the border into the Republic of Cyprus.

Customs formalities are usually minimal, although there are sometimes long waits for passport control. Your luggage may be opened for inspection.

All travelers may import the following without paying import duty: 200 cigarettes or 100 cigarillos or 50 cigars or 250g of smoking tobacco; 1 liter of liquor or 2 liters of fortified wines and 2 liters of other wines; and one bottle of perfume (not exceeding 0.6 liters) and toilet water (not exceeding 0.25 liters).

Currency Restrictions There is no limit on the amount of foreign or local currency you may bring into Cyprus. You may export foreign currency up to the equivalent of US$1,000. No more than C£100 may be taken out of the country. All leftover currency can be exchanged before departure.

| I've nothing to declare. | **Den écho típota na dilóso.** |
| It's for my personal use. | **Íne giá prosopikí chrísi.** |

D

DRIVING

Road Conditions Driving conditions are generally good with well surfaced, well-marked roads and fast expressways running along the south coast linking Limassol, Nicosia, and Larnaca. Beware of speeding on these roads as there are frequent police patrols. Most main roads (shown in orange on maps) are paved and in good condition, and even many of the yellow secondary roads are easily negotiated. Short distances on minor roads (white on maps), typically in the hills, may often be tackled in an ordinary car, but they are usually unpaved and pock-marked with potholes in addition to steep, hairpin turns. You should be alert at all times. Ideally, a 4WD vehicle is best for this kind of driving.

City traffic is fairly orderly. Unless you hit rush hour, you'll encounter only minor traffic jams in Nicosia.

Rules & Regulations British motorists will feel at home in Cyprus, where traffic keeps to the left. Everyone else should go slowly at first, until the habit of driving on the left and overtaking (passing) on the right becomes second nature. Always carry your driver's license and car-rental documents with you.

Speed Limits 50 km/h (30mph) in town, 100 km/h (60mph) on highways.

Fuel Costs Prices compare favorably with those elsewhere in Europe. Diesel fuel is cheaper, and you can rent diesel cars. Filling stations are plentiful around Nicosia, Limassol, Larnaca, Paphos, and the coast, and are rather scarcer in the mountains. If you're setting out on a mountain excursion, be sure the tank is full or nearly so.

Filling stations close on Sundays and holidays, but many have automatic machines that take cash or credit cards. Instructions are provided in English, but they can be a little confusing. If in doubt, wait until a Cypriot driver comes along and he will gladly help you.

Parking This can be a problem in central Nicosia, Limassol, Paphos, and Larnaca. Fines will be handed out if you park illegally. Try to find a metered spot or a parking lot.

Road Distances Distances in km between major tourist centers:

Nicosia–Limassol	82
Nicosia–Larnaca	44
Limassol–Paphos	68
Limassol–Troodos	46
Paphos–Ayia Napa (via coast road)	175
Larnaca–Limassol	66

If You Need Help Always call your car-rental agency first, but failing that, try the Cyprus Automobile Association; Tel. (02) 313233. In an emergency, call the police: Tel. 199.

Cyprus

Road Signs Most are the standard pictographs used throughout Europe, and all written signs are in both English and Greek:

ΑΔΙΕΞΟΔΟΣ	No through road
ΑΛΤ/ΣΤΟΜ	Stop
ΑΝΩΜΑΛΙΑ ΟΔΟΣΤΡΩΜΑΤΟΣ	Bad road surface
ΑΠΑΓΟΡΕΥΕΤΑΙ Η ΑΝΑΜΟΝΗ	No waiting
ΑΠΑΓΟΡΕΥΕΤΑΙ Η ΕΙΣΟΔΟΣ	No entry
ΑΠΑΓΟΡΕΥΕΤΑΙ Η ΣΤΑΘΜΕΥΣΙΣ	No parking
ΔΙΑΒΑΣΙΣΠΕΖΩΝ	Pedestrian crossing
ΕΛΤΤΩΣΑΤΕ ΤΑΧΥΤΗΤΑ	Reduce speed
ΕΠΡΙΚΙΝΔΥΝΗ ΝΟΣ ΚΑΤΩΦΕΡΕΙΑ	Dangerous incline
ΕΡΓΑ ΕΠΙ ΤΗΣ ΟΔΟΥ	Road work in progress
ΚΙΝΔΥΝΟΣ	Caution
ΜΟΝΟΔΡΟΜΟΣ	One-way traffic
ΠΑΡΑΚΑΜΠΤΗΡΙΟΣ	Diversion (detour)
ΠΟΔΗΛΑΤΑΙ	Cyclists
ΠΟΡΕΙΑ ΥΠΟΧΡΕΩΤΙ ΚΗ ΔΕΞΙΑ	Keep right
Are we on the right road for ...?	**Ímaste stososto drómo giá ...?**
Full tank, please. Normal/super/lead-free	**Na to gemísete me venzíni. aplí/soúper/amólivdos**
My car has broken down.	**Épatha mía vlávi.**

There's been an accident.	**Égine éna disteíchima.**
(International) Driving Permit	**(diethnís) ádia odigíseos**
Car registration papers	**ádia kikloforías**
Collision insurance	**asfália enandíon trítou**
Check the oil/tires/battery.	**Na eléchsete ta ládia/ta lá ticha/ti batária.**

ELECTRICITY

The standard current is 240 volts, 50 Hz AC; sockets are usually three-pin, as in the UK. Adapters are available in hotels and shops. Most hotels and apartments have 110-volt outlets for razors.

I need an adapter/battery, please.	**Chriázome éna metaschimatistí/ mia batária, parakaló.**

EMBASSIES & CONSULATES

Australia	High Commission, 4 Annis Komninis Street, Nicosia; Tel. (02) 473001
UK	High Commission, Alexander Palli Street, Nicosia; Tel. (02) 771131, (02) 861100
USA	Embassy, Metochiou and Ploutarchou, Egkomi, Nicosia; Tel. (02) 776400, (02) 776100

EMERGENCIES

Police, Fire Brigade, Ambulance (island-wide) 199

Hospital

Nicosia	(02) 801400, (02) 801475 (ambulance)
Larnaca	(04) 630312, (04) 630300
Limassol	(05) 330777, (03) 330333

Cyprus

Paphos	(06) 240111
Paralimni	(03) 821211
(also for Ayia Napa)	
Polis (also for Latchi)	(06) 321431

These words are useful in difficult situations:

Careful	**Prosochí**	Police	**Astinomía**
Help	**Voíthia**	Stop	**Stamatíste**

G

GETTING THERE (see also AIRPORTS)
For the vast majority of people, air travel is the only practical way of getting to Cyprus.

Direct schedule and charter flights link several British airports to Larnaca and Paphos (4 hours 30 minutes). There are no non-stop flights from North America, but connecting services operate to Larnaca from major cities in North America, including New York, Miami, Los Angeles, and San Francisco. Most Australian travelers to Cyprus fly by way of Athens, Istanbul, or London, while the most direct route from New Zealand is via Milan and Athens. The usual routing to Larnaca from South Africa involves changing planes in Lusaka or Athens.

GUIDES & TOURS

There are various guided coach tours that cover such places as Kykko Monastery and the Troodos Mountains, Paphos, Nicosia, and Kourion. You can also take a two- to three-day cruise to the Holy Land, Egypt, and even Beirut. These are very good value but can be grueling.

The most interesting tours on the island are run by Exalt, who specializes in off-the-beaten-track jeep and trekking expeditions. Devoted to environmentally friendly exploration of the Cypriot wilderness. Their principle geographical area of expertise is the Akamas Peninsula, but they also cover parts of the Troodos. Tel. (06) 243803.

Taxi drivers can also be hired for half-day or full-day tours of the island. Most drivers speak English, and are willing to negotiate a fare for tours.

H

HEALTH & MEDICAL CARE (see also EMERGENCIES)
Medical treatment and assistance is offered free of charge to tourists in case of emergency, but to be completely at ease, take out health insurance to cover any risk of illness and accident while on hjoliday. Your travel agent or insurance company will be able to advise you.

There are very capable doctors and dentists in resorts, cities, and larger towns, as well as good hospital facilities. Your hotel will notify you of the nearest doctor. All doctors are educated abroad and most speak English. Doctors on call on weekends are listed in local newspapers or can be contacted at the following telephone numbers: Tel. 1422 for Nicosia; Tel. 1425 for Limassol; Tel. 1424 for Larnaca; and Tel. 1426 for Paphos.

Stomach upsets should not be a problem, as hotels and restaurants observe high standards of cleanliness. Tap water is safe to drink. The sun can bronze you, but also burn you to a crisp. Take it in very small doses at first and use a sunscreen, particularly if you have delicate skin.

Pharmacies (ΦAPMAKEIO — *farmakío*) are recognized by the sign outside — a red cross on a white background (for opening hours, see page 121). Certain chemists offer 24-hour service — check local newspapers for listings. Most medicines sold in the UK, US, Canada, or in Europe are available, but often require a prescription. Pharmacists can generally advise on minor problems such as cuts, sunburns, blisters, throat infections, and gastric disorders.

Where's the nearest (all-night) pharmacy?	**Pou íne to kondinótero (dianikterévon) farmakio?**
I need a doctor/dentist.	**Chriázome éna giatró/odontogiatró.**
an ambulance	**éna asthenofóro**
a hospital	**nosokomío**

Cyprus

I have...	**Écho...**
a sunburn	**éngavma apó ton ílio**
a headache	**ponokéfalo**
a fever	**piretós**
an upset stomach	**pónos stí kiliá**

HOLIDAYS

In addition to their own national holidays, Cypriots also celebrate certain Greek holidays. Offices close on the following days. Shops remain open on certain holidays: ask locally as to which ones.

1 January	*Protochroniá*	New Year's Day
6 January	*ton Theofaníon*	Epiphany
25 March	*Ikostí Pémti Martíou (tou Evangelismoú)*	Greek National Day
1 April	*Iméra enárxeos kipriakoú*	Greek Cypriot National Day
	agónos giá tin anexartisía	Struggle Day
1 May	*Protomagiá*	Labor Day
15 August	*Dekapentávgoustos (tis Panagías)*	Assumption Day
1 October	*Iméra tis anexartisías (tis Kíprou)*	Cyprus Independence Day
28 October	*Ikostí Ogdói Oktovríou ("Ochi")*	"No" Day, commemorating Greek defiance of Italian invasion of 1940.
24-26 December	*Christoúgenna*	Christmas Eve/Day
26 December	*epávrios ton*	Boxing Day

Movable dates:

Katharí Deftéra	1st Day of Lent/Ash Monday (also known as Green Monday)
Megáli Paraskev	Good Friday
Deftéra tou Páscha	Easter Monday
Kataklyzmós	Pentecost (Festival of the Flood)

Note: The dates on which the movable holidays are celebrated correspond to the Greek Orthodox calendar, and therefore often differ from the dates of the same holidays in other European countries.

Are you open tomorrow?　　**'Iste aniktí ávrio?**

LANGUAGE

English is spoken almost as a dual language in all the resorts, and is understood by the vast majority of the population of the Republic of Cyprus. It is only well off the beaten track that a familiarity with Greek is useful, and even here somebody invariably knows someone who speaks English.

Road signs and most other signs imparting general information appear in both Greek and English all over Cyprus.

The Greek alphabet does not need to be a mystery to you. The table below lists the Greek letters in their capital and small forms, followed by the letter to which they correspond in English.

A	α	a	as in b**ar**
B	β	v	
Γ	γ	g	as in "**go**"*
Δ	δ	d	like **th** in "**th**is"
E	ε	e	as in "g**e**t"
Z	ζ	z	
H	ή	i	like **ee** in "m**ee**t"
Θ	θ	th	as in "**th**in"
I	ι	i	like **ee** in "m**ee**t"
K	κ	k	

Cyprus

Λ	λ	l	
Μ	μ	m	
Ν	ν	n	
Ξ	ξ	x	like **ks** in "than**ks**"
Ο	ο	o	as in "g**o**t"
Π	Π	p	
Ρ	ρ	r	
Σ	σ, ς	s	as in "ki**ss**"
Τ	τ	t	
Υ	υ	i	like **ee** in "m**ee**t"
Φ	φ	f	
Χ	χ	ch	as in Scottish "lo**ch**"
Ψ	ψ	ps	as in ti**ps**y
<u>Ο</u>/Ω	ω	o	as in "g**o**t"
ΟΥ	ου	oo	as in "s**oo**p"
			Except before **i-** and **e**-sounds, when it's pronounced like **y** in "yes."

If you want to try Greek, consult the Berlitz *Greek Phrase Book and Dictionary.* It covers practically all the situations you're likely to encounter during your Cyprus travels.

Here are a few phrases you'll want to use often:

Hello	**Yásoo (informal), Yásas (formal)**
Good morning	**Kaliméra**
Please	**Parakaló**
Good afternoon/evening	**Kalispéra**
Thank you	**Efcharistó**
Good night	**Kaliníkta**
Goodbye	**Chérete**

And here are two phrases that you will only need off the beaten track:

Do you speak English?	**Miláte angliká?**
I don't speak Greek.	**Den miló elliniká.**

M

MAPS

The Cyprus Tourism Organization provides comprehensive island maps and town plans of Nicosia, Limassol, Larnaca, Paphos, Ayia Napa/Protaras, and the Troodos region free of charge to visitors.

There are numerous road maps on sale, most of which are of a uniformly reasonable quality. Try to find the most up-to-date, though even they may not include all new roads and improvements to existing ones. Bookshops in Nicosia, downtown Limassol, and Ktima (Upper Paphos) are the likeliest places for finding up-to-date maps. (Most resorts lack good bookshops.) The best road map is the Marco Polo Shell map, available in the UK.

I'd like a street plan of...	**Tha íthela éna odikó chárti tis...**
a road map of this region	**éna chárti aftís tis periochís**

MEDIA

Newspapers & Magazines

There is a good selection of European periodicals and major American weekly newsmagazines in larger towns. Foreign newspapers generally arrive a day after publication. The *Cyprus Mail*, an English-language daily, has current news coverage and a good one-page "What's On" section which expands to two pages in its sister paper The *Sunday Mail*.

The *Cyprus Weekly* (also in English) carries lively features and helpful information. Most resorts have some sort of free "What's On" magazine that also can be picked up at the tourist office or at participating bars and nightspots.

Have you any English-language newspapers?	**Échete anglikés efimerídes?**

Radio & TV

The Cyprus Broadcasting Corporation (CyBC) transmits English-language programs on FM91 with a bulletin at 10am. News and magazine programs are broadcast from 1:30 to 3pm and from 7pm or 8pm (depending upon the season) until midnight. The BBC World Service transmits daily from 6am to 2:15am. Radio BFBS (British Forces Broadcasting Service) is on the air 24 hours a day with news, music, and chat. Some hotels can receive BBC Radio Five Live.

Nearly all hotels with three or more stars offer cable and satellite television channels, including CNN and Sky. Popular sporting events and British football (soccer) matches can be watched on television in the bars of resorts that subscribe to Sky Sports and/or BBC.

MONEY (see also OPENING HOURS)

Currency The Cyprus pound (C£) is divided into 100 cents.
Coins: 1, 2, 5, 10, 20, and 50 cents
Banknotes: C£1, 5, 10, and 20
For currency restrictions, see CUSTOMS AND ENTRY REQUIREMENTS.

Currency Exchange Hotels change money and travelers' checks, but banks (ΤΡΑΠΕΖΑ, *trápeza*) give much better rates — although the formalities can take longer.

ATMs The easiest method of obtaining cash is through an ATM machine. You'll find ATMs in all resorts and major towns. Depending upon your own individual card charges, this might also be the cheapest way of obtaining money.

Travelers' Checks Eurocheques are in widespread use in Cyprus. Travelers' checks, widely accepted, are best cashed at a bank.

Credit Cards Major credit cards are welcome as payment in most city shops, hotels, and restaurants, as well as by all the international and local car-rental firms. Don't forget to take along your passport to use as identification.

Cash Pounds sterling and other strong currencies may be accepted by shops or restaurants — but you'll probably get a poor exchange rate. You'll want to carry some cash with you, particularly for dining out. Many of the restaurants and tavernas listed in this guide take cash only.

I want to change some pounds/dollars.	**Thélo n alláxo merikés líres/meriká dollária.**
Do you accept travelers' checks?	**Pérnete "travelers' checks"?**
Can I pay with this credit card?	**Boró na plirόso me aftí ti pistotikí kárta?**

OPENING HOURS

National Museums and Archaeological Sites Open year-round Monday–Saturday 9am–5pm, Sunday 10am–1pm. Other museums keep similar but usually shorter hours, and may be closed on Saturday afternoon and all-day Sunday (see page 121 for opening hours of the most important museums).

Banks Monday–Friday 8:15am–12:30pm during July and August. At other times of year, Monday–Friday 8:30am–12:30pm, reopening on Mondays only 3:15–4:45pm. Some banks in tourist centers open for currency exchange only, from 4–7pm (summer) and 3–6pm (winter).

Pharmacies Except for the chemists on 24-hour duty, shops are open Monday–Friday 7:30 or 8am–1:00pm and 3 or 4–7pm (mornings only on Wednesday and Saturday).

Post Offices Generally open Monday–Friday 7:30am–1:30pm. The main post office in Nicosia is open later in summer.

Restaurants Lunch is normally served from approximately 12:30–3pm and dinner from around 7–11:30pm; many restaurants of the less formal kind are open throughout the day, especially in the resorts. Some continue to serve until after midnight.

Shops In summer, spring, and autumn, the siesta is still observed in traditional shops. Most establishments are open Monday–Saturday 8am–1pm and 4–7pm (closing half an hour earlier or later depending upon season). There is no afternoon reopening on Wednesday and

Saturday year-round. From October to April, there is no afternoon break and closing time is around 6pm.

P

PHOTOGRAPHY

For security reasons, you are not allowed to photograph military installations — especially along the border of the Turkish-controlled zone. If you cross to Northern Cyprus, be especially aware of this, as there are even more restricted areas there.

Photography inside museums and churches with ancient icons is usually prohibited, though you may be permitted to take pictures without a flash. Don't be tempted to sneak a picture in places like Kykko Monastery, as you could be unceremoniously frogmarched to the door!

As a matter of courtesy, always ask permission before attempting to photograph people, particularly monks and older people.

I'd like some film for this camera.	**Tha íthela éna film giaftí tí michaní.**
black-and-white film	**asprómavro film**
color film	**énchromo film**
color slides	**énchromo film giá thiafánies**
35-mm film	**éna film triánda pénde milimétr**
How long will it take (to develop)?	**Póte tha íne étimo?**
May I take a picture?	**Boró na páro mía fotografía?**

PLANNING YOUR TRIP ON THE WEB

The official web site of the Cyprus Tourism Organization is <www.cyprustourism.org>. It's quite an entertaining site and provides basic information on several aspects of the island, though nothing in great detail. Another site worth checking out is <www.windowoncyprus.com>, which carries mostly advertisements of local businesses (such as baby-sitting services and sports equipment rental shops), but also provides information about special events in various popular locations.

POLICE

You probably won't see many policemen, but they are around and they invariably prove friendly and helpful. You'll recognize the traffic police by their white gloves and sleeves. The Port Police sport blue uniforms. Regular police officers also wear blue and cruise around in blue-and-white police cars. They all speak some English. Island-wide, the police emergency number is Tel. 199.

Where's the nearest police station?	**Pou íne to kondinótero astinomikó tmíma?**

POST OFFICES

The district post office, to be found in all the resort towns, is open Monday–Friday 7:30am–1:30pm and 3–6pm (except on Wednesday afternoon). On Saturday, they are open from 8:30–10:30am. In July and August, afternoon hours are 4–7pm (also closed on Wednesday afternoon). All other post offices are open Monday to Friday, mornings only, except for Thursday afternoons when they reopen from 3–6pm.

A postcard to Europe costs 26c, to the US 31c, to Australia and New Zealand 36c. Stamps may also be bought at hotels, newsstands, and kiosks. The service to Europe is quite speedy, with postcards arriving within a week or less.

Where's the (nearest) post office/telephone office?	**Pou íne to kodinótero tachidromío/CYTA?**
A stamp for this letter/postcard, please.	**Éna grammató simo giaftó to grámma/graftí tin kárta, parakaló.**
express (special delivery)	**exprés**
airmail	**aeroporikós**
registered	**sistiméno**

PUBLIC TRANSPORTATION

Cyprus has no railway system and the bus service is not always frequent or reliable. Private and shared taxis fill the transportation gap.

Cyprus

Private Taxis Vehicles are metered and rates are low, making private taxis a favorite form of transportation. Many visitors, daunted by the difficult road conditions, travel around the island exclusively by taxi.

Shared Taxis and Mini-buses These take from 4–8 passengers and connect all major towns every half hour. Ask the tourist office for a schedule. Prices are fixed and very reasonable, so this is a good way to get around the island on a budget. You can hail a taxi on the street or call for one by telephone. The numbers of the various private companies are listed in the telephone directory.

Where can I get a taxi/ shared taxi/ mini-bus?	**Pou boró na vro éna taxí/ epivatikó taxí/ mikro poúlman?**
May I have a place on this taxi for…?	**Thélo mía thési sto taxí giá…?**
What's the fare to...?	**Piá íne i timí giá...?**

 R

RELIGION

Southern Cyprus is almost 100 percent Greek Orthodox. The few mosques that you will see are reminders of the days before partition in 1974. Some are still used by Arab communities, however. Despite the North-South divide, there is religious tolerance in the south toward Muslims. The north of the island is strictly Muslim.

You must dress modestly to visit both churches and monasteries. The dress code for the latter is usually rigidly enforced and specifies long trousers for men, a long skirt for women, and covered shoulders for both sexes. Churches are less formal. As long as you are not wearing swimwear or showing a lot of flesh, there is usually no problem. You must remove your shoes before entering a mosque.

T

TAXIS (see PUBLIC TRANSPORTATION)

TELEPHONE

To call Cyprus from abroad, dial 00357, then the number.

To call the UK from Cyprus, dial 0044 plus the area code (omitting the first 0), then the number. To call the US and Canada, dial 001, then the area code, then the number.

Street telephones can be used for local and international calls. All have instructions in English. A phone card, available in C£3, C£5, and C£10 denominations, is by far the easiest way to make international calls.

In most hotels, you can dial long distance from your room, but charges can be exorbitant. Standard rates and other information are available from long-distance operators, all of whom speak perfect English (Tel. 194).

The direct-dialing codes to main Cypriot cities are: Nicosia, Tel. 02; Limassol, Tel. 05; Paphos/Latchi, Tel. 06; Larnaca, Tel. 04; and Ayia Napa/Protaras, Tel. 03.

TIME DIFFERENCES

The chart below shows the time differences between Cyprus and various cities in winter (GMT + 2 hours). In summer, Cypriot clocks are put forward 1 hour, so the time difference with the UK stays the same.

New York	London	**Cyprus**	Johannesburg	Sydney	Auckland
5am	10am	**noon**	noon	9pm	11pm.

What time is it?   **Ti óra íne?**

TIPPING

Service charges are included in hotel, restaurant, and taverna bills. But a little extra is always appreciated, especially for good service.
Average tips:

Hotel porter, per bag	50c–C£1
Maid, per day	C£1
Waiter/barman	15%
Taxi driver	10 percent
Tour guide (private)	around 10%

Cyprus

Tour guide (group tour)	from C£1 per day
Hair stylist/barber	10%

TOILETS

Public conveniences exist in larger towns, but not in great numbers. Museums often have the cleanest facilities, and the ones on the government-run "tourist beaches" are excellent, but overall standards are reasonable.

Toilets are generally indicated in English and Greek, with silhouettes of men and women. If you use the facilities in cafés, restaurants, and hotels, it is customary to buy something.

Where are the toilets?   **Pou íne ta apohoritíra?**

TOURIST INFORMATION

The Cyprus Tourism Organization, or CTO (*Kypriakós Organismós Tourismoú–KOT*) is a gold mine of information, with free brochures and maps. Its staff readily fields all your questions and is quite knowledgeable.

UK   17 Hanover Street, London, W1R 0HB;
         Tel. (0207) 569-8800; fax (0207) 499-4935;
         e-mail: ctolon@ctolon.demon.co.uk

USA   13 E 40th Street, New York, NY 10016;
         Tel. (212) 683-5280; fax (212) 683-5282;
         e-mail: gocyprus@aol.com

For information on Northern Cyprus:

UK   29 Bedford Square, London, WC1B 3EG;
         Tel. (0207) 631-1930; fax (0207) 631-1873
         e-mail: northcyprus@compuserve.com

USA   21 United Nations Plaza, 6th Floor, New York, NY
         10017; Tel. (212) 687- 2350.

         1667 K Street, Suite 590, Washington DC, 20006;
         Tel. (202) 887-6198; fax (202) 467-0685.

In the Republic of Cyprus, the CTO maintains offices at Larnaca airport, open 24 hours (Tel. [04] 643000); Paphos Airport (to meet flights, Tel. [06] 422833); and in the major tourist centers:

Nicosia 11 Aristokyprou Street, Laiki Yitonia; Tel. (02) 674264.

Limassol 15 Spyrou Araouzou Street; Tel. (05) 362756.

Larnaca Plateia Vasileos Pavlou; Tel. (04) 654322.

Paphos 3 Gladstone Street, Ktima; Tel. (06) 232841 (expected to move in 2000).

Ayia Napa 12 Kryou Nerou Avenue; Tel. (03) 721796.

The main office for information on the Troodos area can be found in the center of Platres; Tel. (05) 421316.

In Northern Cyprus, there are offices in Kyrenia (Ziya Rizki Caddesi), Famagusta (Fevzi Cakmak Bulvari), and Nicosia (at the Kyrenia Gate), but opening hours are erratic and the standard of information is so poor as to make them not worth a visit.

Where's the tourist office?   **Pou íne to grafío tourismoú?**

W

WATER

Tap water is safe to drink, and still and sparkling mineral waters are bottled on Cyprus; imported waters are available too.

a bottle of mineral water   **éna boukáli metallikó neró**

fizzy (carbonated)/still   **me/chorís anthrakikó**

WEIGHTS & MEASURES

Liters have superseded gallons — with one sturdy exception: beer is still drunk by the pint.

Cyprus

Length

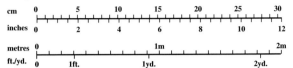

Weight

Temperature

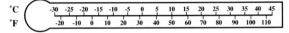

YOUTH HOSTELS

Only members of the International Youth Hostels Association may stay at Cyprus's youth hostels:

Nicosia 5 I. Hadjidakis Street; Tel. (02) 674808 or (02) 670027.

Paphos 37 E. Venizelos Avenue; Tel. (06) 232588.

Troodos Troodos Hill Resort (summer only); Tel. (05) 422400.

Larnaca 27 Nikolaou Rossou Street (near St. Lazarus Church); Tel. (04) 621188.

For further information, contact the Cyprus Youth Hostels Association, PO Box 21328, Nicosia, Cyprus; Tel. (02) 670027.

Some Useful Expressions

hello	**yasoo (informal), yasas (formal)**
yes/no	**ne/óchi**
please/thank you	**parakaló/efcharistó**
excuse me/you're welcome	**me sinchoríte/parakaló**
where/when/how	**pou/póte/pos**
how long/how far	**póso keró/póso makriá**
yesterday/today/tomorrow	**chthes/símera/ávrio**
day/week/month/year	**iméra/evdomáda/mínas/chrónos**
left/right	**aristerá/dexiá**
up/down	**epáno/káto**
good/bad	**kalós/kakós**
big/small	**megálos/mikrós**
cheap/expensive	**ftinós/akrivós**
open/closed	**aniktós/klistós**
here/there	**edó/ekí**
free (vacant)/occupied	**eléftheri/kratiméni**
early/late	**norís/argá**
easy/difficult	**éfkolos/dískolos**
Does anybody here speak English?	**Milá kanís angliká?**
What does this mean?	**Ti siméni aftó?**
I don't understand.	**Den katalavéno.**
Please write it down.	**Parakaló grápste to.**
Is there an admission charge?	**Prépi na pliróso ísodo?**
Waiter, please!	**Garsóni (garçon), parakaló!**
I'd like...	**Tha íthela...**
How much is that?	**Póso káni aftó?**
Have you something less expensive?	**Échete káti ftinótero?**
What time is it?	**Ti óra íne?**
Just a minute.	**Éna leptó.**

Recommended Hotels

All Cyprus hotels are classified by the Cyprus Tourism Organization (CTO) from zero to five stars. Apartments featured below are all Class A, the CTO's highest grade.

Be aware that as Cyprus is heavily geared towards package tourism, many hotels are block booked by big operators. Reservations made as far in advance as possible are always advisable. The Cyprus Hotel Association's desk at Larnaca International Airport can assist incoming passengers with reservations. The CTO's offices at Larnaca International Airport, Paphos International Airport, and Limassol Harbor can also make bookings. For booking from aboard, the Cyprus country code is 00357.

Unless otherwise specified, all 4- and 5-star hotels have at least one restaurant, one swimming pool, and one tennis court. Rooms feature satellite television and a minibar/fridge, plus 24-hour room service.

All hotels listed below offer meal plans: bed and breakfast (b and b), half board (breakfast plus dinner or lunch), or full board (three meals daily). The minimum is usually b and b.

Beachfront hotels in Cyprus are very much alike. All achieve an acceptable international standard, but the rooms can be bland. If the rooms are particularly appealing, this is noted in the entries that follow. All beachfront hotels offer water sports. Air-conditioning is standard in all but the most basic accommodations. As a basic guide to room prices, we have used the following symbols (high season, double room, including breakfast):

$$$$$	above CY£160
$$$$	C£111-C£160
$$$	C£81-C£110
$$	C£50-C£80
$	below C£50

All establishments listed below take major credit cards.

Nicosia

Averof $ *19 Averof Street; Tel. (02) 463447; fax (02) 773411.* This friendly Anglo-Cypriot family-run two-star hotel is one of the best budget choices in town. It is a 10- to 15-minute walk from the old town walls and a ten-minute walk to the municipal swimming pool. 25 rooms.

Best Western Classic $$ *Regaena Street; Tel. (02) 664006; fax (02) 360072.* This small hotel enjoys a convenient location just within the city walls near the Paphos Gate, a five-minute walk from the old Ledra Palace checkpoint. It has an attractive lounge area, small but comfortable bedrooms, a lively cocktail bar, an excellent restaurant (Fifty Nine Knives, see page 139) and a small but well-equipped gym, all of which belie its humble two-star rating. The young staff is very friendly and professional. 57 rooms.

Cyprus Hilton $$$$$ *Archbishop Makarios Avenue; Tel. (02) 377777; fax 377788; e-mail <hiltoncy@spidernet.com.cy>* This luxury five-star hotel is the city's top meeting point, set in a relatively quiet setting back from the main road, a five-minute drive from the old town. It offers a choice of three restaurants and excellent sports facilities including a swimming pool, tennis courts, and health club. Wheelchair access. 298 rooms.

Holiday Inn Nicosia $$$ *70 Regaena Street; Tel. (02) 475131; fax (02) 473337.* Renovated in the mid-1990s to a very high standard, this four-star hotel features its own swimming pool and health club. Very good location just within the city walls near the Paphos Gate, a five-minute walk from the old Ledra Palace checkpoint. 140 rooms.

Larnaca

Flamingo Beach $ *Piale Pasha Street; Tel. (04) 650621; fax (04) 656732.* This family-run three-star seafront hotel lies on the southern edge of town, just after the fort and right by the start of Mackenzie Beach. All rooms have a seaview balcony. Rooftop pool. 64 rooms.

Golden Bay $$$$ *Larnaca–Dhekelia Road; Tel. (04) 645444; fax (04) 645451.* This luxury five-star beachfront hotel lies 8km (5 miles) east of town and is set in landscaped water-theme gardens. Rooms and suites are of a very high standard, all recently renovated. Excellent leisure and health and beauty facilities including an outdoor jacuzzi. 194 rooms.

Sandy Beach $$ *Larnaca–Dhekelia Road; Tel. (04) 646333; fax (04) 646900.* Friendly, large four-star beachfront hotel on Larnaca Bay 7 km (4–5 miles) east of town with tavernas, bars, and restaurants within walking distance. Renovated in 1998. Indoor and outdoor swimming pools, good health club, and fully equipped gym. 205 rooms.

Sun Hall $$ *Athens Avenue; Tel. (04) 653341; fax (04) 652717.* This medium-sized four-star hotel is right in the center of the action on the main Palm Tree Promenade, opposite the beach and marina. Health club and gym, but no pool. 112 rooms.

Ayia Napa & Region

Asterias Beach $$ *Makronissos, Ayia Napa; Tel. (03) 721901; fax (03) 722095.* Set on the outskirts of town on the beautiful popular sandy beach of Makronissos, this well-equipped four-star hotel has its own swimming pool, tennis courts, and many other high-quality facilities. 172 rooms.

Cornelia $ *23 Makarios Avenue Ayia Napa; Tel. (03) 721406; fax (03) 723578.* Good-value, small, two-star bed-and-breakfast hotel with a swimming pool, restaurant, and baby-sitting service. 28 rooms.

Grecian Bay $$$ *Ayia Napa; Tel. (03) 721301; fax (03) 721307; web site <www.grecian.com.cy>*. Large five-star hotel in a good location — a ten-minute walk east of the town center — set on a lovely stretch of golden sandy beach with shallow water. Amenities include indoor and outdoor swimming pools, tennis, water sports facilities, and a discotheque. 271 rooms.

Grecian Park $$$ *Konnos Bay, Protaras; Tel. (03) 832000; fax (03) 832870; e-mail <grecian-park-hotel@cytanet.com.cy>*. Set halfway between Ayia Napa and Protaras on the edge of the National Park, this excellent five-star hotel enjoys a wonderful hilltop location overlooking the beautiful sandy beach of Konnos Bay. In addition to the usual facilities, it features luxurious public areas, a large free-form swimming pool, and a grassy sunbathing terrace with great sea views. 245 rooms.

Nausica Beach $$ *Protaras; Tel. (03) 831160; fax (03) 831519*. These classy low-rise apartments enjoy a great location on a promontory overlooking beautiful Fig Tree Bay and the island's best sandy beaches. Accommodation is spacious, comfortable, and stylish with a whitewashed Mediterranean theme. All the facilities of a good four-star hotel. 192 units.

Limassol

Ajax $$ *Corner of Damon and D. Nikolaou streets, Mesa Yitonia; Tel. (05) 590000; fax (05) 591222; e-mail <ajakhtl@logos.cy.net>* This large, modern four-star hotel is set between the tourist area of Potamos Yermasoyias and the town center, some 800 meters away from the beach. Facilities include outdoor and indoor pools, floodlit tennis courts, a health club, and a children's club. 176 rooms.

Amathus Beach $$$$ *Amathus; Tel. (05) 321152; fax (05) 327494; web site <www.amathus-hotel.com>*. This five-star beachfront hotel set 9 km (6 miles) east of the city center is a member of the Leading Hotels of the World group. Its extensive landscaped grassy grounds include two swimming pools, one of which features underwater music! In the summer, the hotel runs its own beachside fish taverna. 244 rooms.

Le Meridien $$$$ *Old Limassol–Nicosia Road, Amathus; Tel. (05) 634000; fax: (05) 634222; e-mail <meridien@ zenon.logos.cy.new>.* Superb five-star hotel some 12 km (8 miles) east of town. Set in its own spacious secluded gardens with a large free-shaped pool, Le Meridien has 300 meters (1,000 ft) of beach frontage. A boardwalk offers romantic moonlit walks. Rooms are very spacious, all with large balconies and equipped to the highest standards. Meals, particularly breakfast, are excellent, with the rustic Village Taverna providing a very good imitation of a real Cypriot taverna. Comprehensive sports, health and beauty facilities, and a very popular children's club set in its own "village." Wheelchair access. 295 rooms.

Troodos Mountains

Churchill Pinewood Valley $$ *Pedhoulas; Tel. (02) 952211; fax (02) 952439.* Set between Pedhoulas and Prodhromos, this three-star mountain lodge-style hotel is set in its own lovely secluded cherry orchard and pine forest with landscaped gardens and a tea terrace. Rooms are comfortable and tastefully decorated. Swimming pool (open May-October), tennis court, gym, sauna, and children's playground. 50 rooms.

Forest Park Hotel $$ *Pano Platres; Tel. (02) 421751; fax (02) 421875; e-mail <forest@cytanet.com.cy>.* Renovated in 1998 and nestling in its own forest, the four-star Forest Park offers many of the creature comforts of its beachside counterparts, including a heated outdoor pool (open May-October) and an indoor pool. It also has the bonus of being within walking distance of Pano Platres village. 140 rooms.

Linos Inn \$ *Old Kakopetria 34, Kakopetria; Tel. (02) 923161, fax (02) 923181.* This beautifully restored complex of old village houses, opened in 1997, offers a romantic and homey setting with lots of antique fittings and furnishings. Facilities include mini-bars and satellite TVs, sauna, and jacuzzi. Half board may be obligatory mid-July to mid-September, but this is no hardship as the Linos Inn also features a very attractive traditional restaurant serving excellent food. 7 rooms.

Paphos & Region

Alexander the Great \$\$\$ *Poseidon Avenue, Paphos; Tel. (06) 265000; fax (06) 265100; e-mail <alexander@ kanika-group.com>.* Located on the best stretch of town beach, this four-star hotel is close to all town center activities. Good sporting facilities include outdoor and indoor pools and tennis courts. Health and beauty club. 202 rooms.

Aliathon Village \$\$ *Poseidon Avenue, Yeroskipou; Tel. (06) 264400; fax (06) 264700.* Set some 2 km (1 mile) from town, and just 200 meters from the nearest beach, this attractive bungalow complex is set around a pool and lawns. It has all the facilities of a large three- or four-star hotel but on a smaller scale. Rooms are tastefully furnished in pale wood and feature Mediterranean styling. Good sports facilities including pool and tennis court. Excellent value. 63 bungalows.

Annabelle \$\$\$\$\$ *Poseidon Avenue, Paphos; Tel. (06) 238333; fax (06) 245402; e-mail <thanos.hotels@spidernet.com.cy>.* This refined luxury five-star beachfront hotel is in the center of town overlooking the harbor. Attractive gardens around the pool rooms, renovated in 1997, are large and well-furnished. Good sports facilities. Its main restaurant serves the best steaks in town. 198 rooms.

(Leptos) Coral Beach \$\$\$\$\$ *Coral Beach; Tel. (06) 621601; fax (06) 621900.* Some 12 km (8 miles) north of

Cyprus

Paphos, this highly-rated luxury five-star resort is a perfect place to escape the bustle of town with lush landscaped gardens that open onto a sandy beach. Watersports on the beach plus an extensive range of other leisure facilities, including a health and beauty spa, four floodlit tennis courts, and an archery range. At its innovative arts and crafts center, guests can learn glass painting, pottery, and ceramic painting under expert tuition. Wheelchair access. 304 rooms.

Cynthiana Beach $$ *Kisonerga; Tel. (06) 233900; fax (06) 244648; web site <www.cynthiana-hotel.com>.* This large three-star beachfront hotel is set some 8 km (5 miles) west of town on a headland, in large landscaped gardens flanked by banana plantations and a sandy beach immediately below. Indoor and outdoor swimming pools, tennis courts, and other sports facilities. 198 rooms.

Cypria Maris $$$ *Poseidon Avenue, Yeroskipou; Tel. (06) 264111; fax (06) 264125.<www.cypria-maris.com>* This smart four-star hotel set 3 km east of the harbor features a little more style and character than other comparable Paphos accommodations. Extensive palm-shaded gardens surround the pool and lead directly onto the beach. Wheelchair access. 239 rooms.

Kiniras $ *91 Makarios Avenue; Tel. (06) 241604; fax (06) 242176; web site <www.kiniras.com.cy>.* If you don't need a beachfront setting or four-star luxury, this charming small hotel (rated as a "traditional house" by the CTO) is far and away the best deal in Paphos. The effervescent George and his friendly family do absolutely everything, including preparing superb meals in a beautiful setting (see page 143). The hotel is a traditional 70-year old house with public areas beautifully decorated in rustic style. Rooms are plain but comfortable. Located on the upper town's main street, it is very quiet at night. No pool but the municipal baths are just 200 meters (600 ft) away. 18 rooms.

Laura Beach $$$$ *Paphos–Coral Bay Road, Chlorakas; Tel. (06) 244900; fax (06) 244911; e-mail <laura@cytanet.com.cy>*. The highly regarded four-star Laura Beach stands 5 km (3 miles) north of Paphos in extensive grounds with a large pool and lush greenery. Immediately below is a good sandy beach. Rooms are large if slightly dated, but public areas are very attractive with lots of marble and potted plants. All-inclusive packages available. 292 rooms.

Paphian Bay $$ *Poseidon Avenue, Yeroskipou; Tel. (06) 264333; fax (06) 264870*. Opened in 1988, this three-star hotel is set in spacious landscaped grounds on one of Paphos's nicest stretches of beach — a quiet spot some 3 km (2 miles) from town. Rooms are attractively decorated. Guests in search of more facilities can make free use of those at its four-star sister property (Pioneer Beach, see below) next door. Good value. 219 rooms (all with sea views).

Pioneer Beach $$$ *Poseidon Avenue, Yeroskipou; Tel. (06) 264500; fax (06) 264370*. This large four-star hotel is a five-minute ride south of Paphos center on one of the town's best stretches of sand. Nicely furnished modern comfortable rooms. 255 rooms.

Roman $$ *Agios Lambrianos Street; Tel. (06) 245411; fax (06) 246834*. Set 1 km (^{1}/$_2$ mile) from the town center and a five-minute walk from the beach, the three-star Roman looks like a genuine ancient monument from the outside while the interior is a daring and fanciful exercise in ancient Roman-theme décor. Bold and breezy wall paintings, colorful mosaics, and "Roman" paraphernalia dominate all public areas and bedrooms. Small but attractive swimming pool. Its smaller twin sister, the three-star Melina just around the corner, provides a very similar experience. 87 rooms.

Recommended Restaurants

We appreciated the food and service in the restaurants listed below. If you find other places worth recommending, we would be pleased to hear from you. During the summer season, restaurants that are open all day generally operate from 9:30am–11pm. Those which only serve lunch and dinner are usually open from 12–3pm and 6:30–11:30pm. If you are planning a special journey to a place in low season, it's always advisable to call ahead to confirm opening hours, as some places close early or open late out of season.

Average meal prices, which are controlled by the government, are remarkably uniform (though fish dishes are more expensive), so don't be surprised to find that most places listed below fall into the moderate price bracket. Prices relate to a three-course meal (or a *meze*) per person, excluding drinks.

\$\$\$	above C£9
\$\$	C£6–9
\$	below C£6

Credit cards are **not** accepted unless otherwise indicated.

Nicosia & Northern Cyprus

Abu Faysal \$\$ *31 Klementos Street, Nicosia; Tel. (02) 360353.* Open daily for lunch and dinner. Excellent Lebanese food served in a relaxing atmosphere, especially in warm weather when the garden (which also serves as an art gallery) is open. Jazz on occasional nights in winter.

Arhondiko \$\$ *27 Aristokyprou Street, Laiki Yitonia, Nicosia; Tel. (02) 450080.* Open all day Monday to Saturday, from 5pm on Sunday. Pretty little restaurant in a romantic setting with tables under the trees in the heart of the restored, pedestrian Laiki Yitonia. Try the traditional *meze*, stuffed vegetables, quail, pilaf, or push the boat out with gilthead sea bream.

Canli Balik $$ *Kyrenia Harbor; Tel. (90 392) 8152182.* Open daily lunch and dinner. Probably the best of the many fish restaurants on this splendid harbor, Canli Balik enjoys an elevated center stage view and serves consistently good fish dishes. Ideal for lunch.

Fifty Nine Knives $$-$$$ *Best Western Classic Hotel. 94 Rigenis Street, Nicosia; Tel. (02) 464006.* Open daily for lunch and dinner (closed for dinner August). The name refers to an archaeological find below the present building, not what's in the cutlery drawer, and this excellent little restaurant is a find itself. Ultra modern and very stylish without being intimidating, it serves innovative "Modern Cypriot" dishes with an international twist, as well as some interesting international dishes at very reasonable prices. You can go for a "small plate" or a "large plate," depending on your appetite. Major credit cards accepted.

Matheos/Matheus (ΜΑΤΘΑΙΟΣ) $ *Plateia Ikostiogdhois Oktovriou, Nicosia; Tel. (02) 755846.* Open daily all day. A no-frills locals' place that's recommended by everyone but is used to tourists. They serve all the usual favorites, but try something seasonal, such as quail or rabbit with pilaf. It's easy to find (at the back of the Fanoremeni Church by the tiny mosque), with outdoor and indoor seating.

Larnaca

1900 Art Cafe $$ *6 Stasinou Street; Tel. (04) 653027.* Open daily from 6pm–midnight. Charming, arty café-restaurant set in a lovely turn-of-the-century house just opposite the Pierides Museum. Downstairs, among the artworks, drinks and snacks are served, while upstairs is an excellent, inventive restaurant. Home-cooked dishes include chicken in honey and lemon; chicken in beer; chicken with orange juice, thyme, and garlic; *tavas*; stuffed vegetables; and other vegetarian options. The café is run by a local radio celebrity, and on Friday evenings university students may contribute live music.

Militzis $$ *42 Piale Pasha Street; Tel. (04) 655867 or (04) 665113.* Open daily noon–midnight. Just south of the old fort, Militzis is marked by the windmill on its front terrace. A short but gutsy, meat-only menu features such no-nonsense dishes as *kokoretsi* (offal), *zalatina* (brawn/jellied pork), *kefalaki* (lamb's head), and more conventional grills and casseroles in generous portions. *Kleftiko* is a house specialty. Takeout is available.

Vassos Varoshiotis Fish Taverna $$ *7 Piale Pasha Street, corner of Sakarya Street; Tel. (04) 655865.* Open daily for lunch and dinner. One of the best fish tavernas in town, it has been catering to locals as well as visitors since 1964. Try the fish meze.

Ayia Napa & Region

Konatjin $$ *15 Ayia Thomas Street (opposite St Marinas church), Paralimni; Tel. (03) 828359.* Open daily for lunch and dinner. It's well worth the short trip from Protaras or Ayia Napa to get away from resort life and to taste the excellent Greek-style meze at this traditional taverna.

Limelight Taverna $$ *Lipertis Street (opposite the post office), Ayia Napa; Tel. (03) 721650.* Open daily all day. The best grill house in town for steaks, but also recommended for lamb, suckling pig, and *souvlaki*, all cooked over charcoal.

Oleander $$ *Kryou Nerou Avenue, Agia Napa; Tel. (03) 721951.* Open daily all day. A few steps away from the tourist office, the long-established Oleander is one of the few traditional Cypriot restaurants in the center of town. Good food and service.

To Ploumin $$ *3 28th Octovriou Street, Sotira; Tel. (09) 658333 or (03) 730444.* Usually open daily for lunch and dinner, but check in advance. This charming traditional taverna of formica-topped table and Van Gogh-style wicker chairs was built in 1938 and is now a listed building. With displays of old tools, pottery, furniture, and handicrafts, it's lovely for a home-cooked meze.

Limassol

The Old Harbor–Ladas Fish Tavern $$-$$$ *Old Harbor; Tel. (05) 365760 or (05) 344100.* Open Monday to Saturday for lunch and dinner. An atmospheric and friendly place at the old port that has been going strong for 50 years, and claims to be the oldest fresh fish tavern in Limassol. It is certainly one of the best, with an excellent selection of the best quality fish straight off the adjacent boats, usually simply grilled over charcoal. Popular with locals and visitors.

Richard and Berengaria $ *23 Eirinis Street. No telephone bookings.* Open daily all day. This is no more than a humble snack bar (look for a forest of colorful yellow-and-white Keo parasols), but it's a perfect place for a quick cheap bite after sightseeing around the castle and old port. Their *sheftalia* is wonderful!

Troodos Mountains

Linos Inn $$-$$ *Old Kakopetria River; Tel. (02) 923161.* Open daily lunch and dinner. A splendidly renovated taverna in an Alpine-like setting of beautifully restored old village houses (see page 135) in the heart of Old Kakopetria. Excellent inventive regional and Cypriot dishes.

Maryland at the Mill $$-$$$ *Kakopetria River; Tel. (02) 922536.* Open daily lunch and dinner. Set on the top floor of a beautifully converted mill, a visit here is an experience in itself. Book a table on the small outside balcony if possible. The local specialty, fresh trout, is almost *de rigueur* here, but the souvlaki and kleftiko are also good.

Psilo Dhendhro $$ *Platres–Limassol Road; Tel. (05) 421350.* Open daily 11am–5pm. With a trout farm on the premises, your choice of meal is decided for you at this very popular and attactive establishment. A perfect place for rest and refreshment after walking the scenic trail to the Kaledonia waterfall, which starts and finishes here (see page 69). Book before you set off.

Paphos & Region

Bagnia (Ta Μπavia) $$ *Poseidon Avenue. Tel: (06) 241558.* Open daily all day. Set right on the seafront in a busy part of town, Bagnia means "the baths," referring to the municipal swimming pool and sea area immediately next door. It's a popular, friendly, and enjoyable place to catch the breeze, and is surprisingly sheltered from the hubbub. The atmosphere is very much that of a bright and breezy blue-and-white Mediterranean seaside café. A wide range of snacks and full meals is on offer, though the quality of the latter is variable.

Cavallini $$$ *Poseidon Avenue (next to Amathus hotel); Tel. (06) 264164.* Open Monday to Saturday from 7pm. Probably the best Italian restaurant in town, Cavallini offers high quality sophisticated dining from an interesting and wide-ranging northern Italian menu on a lovely terrace. Major credit cards accepted.

Chez Alex (Stefanos Fish Restaurant) $$$ *7 Constantias Street (corner of Tefkrou Street), Kato Paphos; Tel. (06) 234767.*Open daily, lunch and dinner. In a quiet part of the central nightlife area, Chez Alex is the town's most highly regarded fish restaurant. If it swims, they cook it — give 3 hours notice for their specials of Surprise Sea Bream (baked in a salt crust) or local *bouillabaisse*; 12 hours notice is required for lobster. Classy nautical-theme dining room with outdoor terrace. Major credit cards accepted.

Demokritos $$ *1 Dionysou Street, Kato Paphos; Tel. (06) 233371.* Open nightly. It's hard to miss Demokritos — just follow the crowds who stand wide-eyed at the amazing after-dinner glass-balancing dancing feats of its staff. Open since 1971, it is the oldest taverna-restaurant in Paphos. These days, it trades more heavily on its music and dancing than its food. The international and local dishes are inevitably compromised due to the large numbers of people served. Nonetheless, this is still a very good night out.

Fettas Corner Restaurant $ *Corner of Iakovidhi and Ioannis Agrotis streets, Ktima (Upper Paphos); Tel. (06) 237822.* Open all day Monday–Saturday. After visiting the nearby museums, it's nice to take a seat under a parasol, either on the street corner, or on the edge of the gardens next to Fettas. Don't look for anything fancy here. Simple grills are the hallmark of this basic, owner-managed locals' restaurant. Service can be slow.

Kiniras $$ *91 Makarios Avenue, Ktima (Upper Paphos); Tel. (06) 241604.* Open daily for lunch and dinner, or for drinks at any time. The garden courtyard of the Kiniras hotel (see page 136) is one of the nicest places for a meal on the island. The food is excellent and portions are hearty. The menu features some inventive international dishes, but ask the effervescent and charming proprietor, George, for his recommendation and you will probably be steered toward a traditional Greek favorite such as kleftiko or *stifado*. Highly recommended. Major credit cards accepted.

Seacrest $$-$$$ *Latchi Harbor; Tel. (06) 321333.* Open daily all day. You probably won't go wrong at any of Latchi's clutch of harborside restaurants, as they all enjoy fish straight from the boat to the kitchen. The Seacrest is among the best of these, with a perfect front-row harbor view. For a splurge, try the Seacrest Special — lobster stuffed with sole and crabmeat. Major credit cards accepted.

Pelican $$$ *The Harbor, Kato Paphos; Tel. (06)246886.* Open daily all day. Occupying a very smart terrace on the harborfront, the Pelican is the best of the several fish restaurants that vigorously compete for customers here. Go for the fish meze or one of the Pelican's many swordfish specials. Major credit cards accepted.

Seagull $$ *7 Poseidon Avenue, Kato Paphos (next to Porto Paphos Hotel). Tel. (06) 250489.* Open Wednesday–Monday all day. Set by the seashore and painted in traditional dark blue-and-white Greek style, the family-run Seagull is a relaxed place for a drink, snack, or full meal. The menu is standard fare (fish is the specialty), but everything is well cooked and served with a smile.

Seven St George's Tavern $ *Yeroskipou, just off the main road to Kato Paphos. Tel. (09) 675173.* Open lunch and dinner Tuesday–Sunday. It's not easy to find this charming garden taverna, but it is well worth the effort. George and Lara, the affable owners, offer the best meze on the island (the only choice you have to make is whether or not you want vegetarian). The quality of the food, the many types of dishes, the service, and the atmosphere are light years away from the anonymous *moussaka*-and-chips joints of Kato Paphos. Beware, the dishes keep on coming until you say stop!

Spondas Fish Tavern $$ *Agias Anastasias, Kato Paphos; Tel. (06) 234131.* Open all day daily. Established in 1983 and set just away from the noisy nightlife area, Spondas is one of the most attractive traditional restaurants in Kato Paphos.